Praise for

the AFROMINIMALIST'S

GUIDE TO LIVING

WITH LESS

"This book is an extraordinary, life-changing invitation to live life on your terms. Christine Platt shows us that minimalism isn't a one-size fits all, colorless lifestyle but instead a way for us to live with intention, letting go of what doesn't matter and surrounding ourselves with what does. With warmth, wisdom, humor, and radical honesty, she takes us on a journey back to the essence of minimalism."

—Courtney Carver, author of *Soulful Simplicity* and *Project 333*

"Though titled a guide, what Platt has created is less of a script or scripture and more of a Rorschach test for each reader—especially those of us who are Black—to see in themselves whatever they need to, in hopes to make living with less, living as more."

—Jason Reynolds, *New York Times* bestselling author

"Christine's book is the one I wish I'd had at my side when I began my own journey to living with less. She is a warm, engaging guide who frames minimalism in a new light—one that examines the why behind our consumption and is more about authenticity than aesthetics. Finally, there is a book about minimalism for people who don't relate to an austere style!"

—Laura Fenton, author of *The Little Book of Living Small*

"Christine has made accessible the very notion of living in a sustainable way from a cultural, historical, and fashionable lens. Her approach to environmentalism is refreshing and necessary and is an important body of work at the intersection of racial and environmental justice."

—Céline Semaan, founder of Slow Factory Foundation

"*Less* is a mindset of expansion, and in *The Afrominimalist's Guide to Living with Less*, Christine Platt gives us a new roadmap to curate the life we've always wanted."

—Kate Northrup, author of *Do Less* and *Money: A Love Story*

"Christine Platt is a natural storyteller. She invites us to reimagine what we think we know about minimalism, our relationship to our belongings, and what we make space for in our lives. These four steps will change your life and gently usher you into your own physical and mental space of sweet simplicity."

—Rachel Cargle, author of *I Don't Want Your Love and Light*

"By detailing her own maximalist-to-minimalist transformation, Platt puts readers at ease—there's no stuff-shaming—with humor and a heavy dose of 'been-there, bought-that, never-worn-it' empathy."

—*The Washington Post*

the AFROMINIMALIST'S
GUIDE TO LIVING
WITH LESS

christine platt

SIMON ELEMENT
new york   london   toronto   sydney   new delhi

SIMON ELEMENT

An Imprint of Simon & Schuster, Inc.
1230 Avenue of the Americas
New York, NY 10020

First Simon Element paperback edition May 2022

SIMON ELEMENT and colophon are trademarks of Simon & Schuster, Inc.

For information about special discounts for bulk purchases,
please contact Simon & Schuster Special Sales at 1-866-506-1949
or business@simonandschuster.com.

The Simon & Schuster Speakers Bureau can bring authors to your
live event. For more information or to book an event, contact
the Simon & Schuster Speakers Bureau at 1-866-248-3049 or visit
our website at www.simonspeakers.com.

Interior design by Michelle Marchese
Illustrations by Octavia Ink

Manufactured in the United States of America

1   3   5   7   9   10   8   6   4   2

Library of Congress Cataloging-in-Publication Data has been applied for.

ISBN 978-1-9821-6804-9
ISBN 978-1-9821-6805-6 (pbk)
ISBN 978-1-9821-6806-3 (ebook)

contents

welcome to the journey   1
meet your guide: the afrominimalist   11

part one: the principles

minimalism: an introduction   33
why you have more than you need   37
why it's so hard to let go   77
a journey without a destination   91

part two: the process

step one: acknowledge you have too much   103
step two: forgive yourself   113
step three: let go!   121
step four: pay it forward   135

part three: the practice

the power of authenticity   147
a lesson in intention   169
less is liberation   196
keep going, keep growing   199

acknowledgments   209
notes   211

For the ancestors. Living with less is now our choice.

afro·min·i·mal·ism

a minimalist life influenced by the African diaspora

welcome to the journey

Once upon a time, not so long ago, no one could have convinced me that I would one day write a guide that encouraged others to pursue a minimalist lifestyle. In fact, if someone had even casually mentioned my name in connection with minimalism, I would have laughed.

Me? *Choosing* to live with less? Ha! I was a bargain shopper. A woman who embraced an I-buy-what-I-want-because-I-deserve-it-especially-if-it's-on-sale philosophy. And I had little desire to change.

Although today I am known as the Afrominimalist, for much of my adulthood living with less was not even on my list of aspirations. I once took pride in my overflowing dressers and closets (yes, plural!) and saw nothing wrong with my life of overindulgence. Paycheck to paycheck, I relished the act of shopping for sport and frequently boasted about my limitless ability to find the best deal. As far as I was concerned, like millions of other Americans, I was living the dream.

I bought things because I could. Because I felt that I deserved to be rewarded. Because I worked hard and had earned the right to purchase whatever I wanted whenever I wanted. Because I believed that certain high-end items were reflections of success and so acquiring designer wares was tangible evidence of my societal standing and self-worth. Because some items were so discounted it seemed criminal *not* to buy them!

This was the pattern of my life as a mindless consumer who acquired things out of habit or want rather than intention or necessity. That is, until the summer of 2016, the first time I was forced to confront and acknowledge the painful reality of my choices. It was the beginning of a fortuitous season of self-discovery, one that would ultimately lead to a lifelong journey of learning to live with less. Because up until then, I had no clue that I owned over fifty pairs of jeans (even though I only wore the same two pairs). I had mastered the art of ignoring the cluttered bins under my bathroom sink, refusing to own up to my obsession with health, beauty, and wellness products (even though I regularly discarded brand-new containers because I was unable to use them before they expired). And I had no idea that my six-year marriage would soon end in divorce, requiring a move from our spacious, two-story marital property in the suburbs to return to the 630-square-foot condo in the city where I had lived as a single woman.

That summer and the months that followed humbled me. I encountered many seemingly insurmountable mountains of hardship. From the painful acknowledgment that I had a lot of expensive things but little savings, to understanding the consequences of failing to prioritize my needs over my wants, the early phases of my journey to minimalism were trials by fire that forced me to accept my overconsumption and wastefulness, and these truths would inevitably lead to my liberation.

Today my journey continues and I am honored to be considered a leading Black minimalist practicioner in a movement that is predominantly White, both literally and figuratively. I had to learn a lot of things the hard way, but I learned. Which is why I feel well-equipped to be *your* guide. Because I truly believe anyone can embrace a lifestyle of less.

You can be a minimalist. Yes, you!

Over the past decade, the word "minimalism" has become so trendy, it can often appear to be yet another form of consumerism. Between the allure of simplistic but often expensive furnishings and conflicting (unofficial) rules about how many things a person can own, what constitutes minimalism is not only confusing at times but it can also seem unattainable. Visuals of neutral colors and vast spaces with few expensive furnishings are often presented as the ideal décor. So, it is not surprising that many people have doubts and fears about their ability to pursue and maintain a minimalist lifestyle.

But it does not have to be this way; it *shouldn't* be this way.

Becoming a minimalist is not about conforming to a particular design style or simplifying your wardrobe. In fact, focusing on serene, austere spaces can distract from the true practice. Living with less is about being a more mindful consumer. At its core, the practice of minimalism asks us to ensure our belongings reflect our truest selves. Or as I often say, "that we only have what we need, use, and love."

Despite appearing complicated, minimalism is quite simple. I can say this with confidence because, well, as I shared, I learned the hard way (see previous page). (Or rather, because I made the practice harder than it needed to be.)

Like so many others in pursuit of simplicity, my journey to less began with online searches and admiring photos on social platforms like Instagram and Pinterest. The beautiful images of clean, tidy spaces left me longing for the lives of the seemingly happy people who occupied them. It was difficult not to be taken with the appeal of minimalism and the joy and ease it promised.

Naively, I thought that if I, too, decluttered and embraced the popular Nordic concept of hygge, I could flip the switch from maximalist to minimalist and live happily ever after with less. I mean, how hard could it be? All I needed to do was paint my walls white, find what "sparked joy," and fill donation bags to ensure I had space for what I truly wanted . . . right?

Wrong!

Letting go of what no longer served me proved to be an arduous task. As I emptied dresser drawers and triaged kitchen cupboards, there were many times it was hard to not feel as if I had been bamboozled, tricked into trying to pursue a lifestyle that was more complicated than effortless. And there were many more times I wondered if I would ever experience the seemingly mythical benefits that minimalist practitioners promised.

As it turned out, my experience is quite common. Often when people think of minimalism, they imagine placing their belongings in huge piles, smiling as they get rid of things they should have discarded long ago or never accepted into their lives at all. At the end, this process somehow magically results in a spotlessly organized home, complete with clean lines, hygge feelings, and the keys to the good life. If only it were that easy.

Let me be clear: Letting go of unused and unloved items *is* part of the process of living with less. But the *practice* of minimalism, what it really takes to achieve and maintain a minimalist lifestyle, involves much more than discarding old T-shirts and buying the perfect storage containers. You can whittle down your belongings to fit into a single carry-on suitcase, but unless you do the work to understand *why* you had so much stuff in the first place and determine what you truly need, use, and love, you'll end up back at square one faster than you think.

For this reason, *The Afrominimalist's Guide to Living with Less* approaches minimalism through the process of self-discovery, of first learning why you have more than you need and then understanding why it's so hard to go. So, don't gather your garbage bags and donation bins just yet. You'll be doing some inner work before the laborious task of letting go begins.

Perhaps you have already tried to adopt a minimalist lifestyle, with little success. Or maybe you find the idea of minimalism intriguing but have no idea what the practice truly means, let alone how or where to start. Regardless of where you are in your journey, I created *The Afrominimalist's Guide to Living with Less* to give you the one thing I found myself longing for when I first began my journey: guidance.

Guidance on understanding why I had more than I needed.

Guidance on what to do in the moment, how to let go, and what to do with the excess.

Guidance on what was to come.

And guidance on how to maintain my new lifestyle.

My hope for you, my dear reader, is not that you come away from this book ready to embrace an Afrominimalist lifestyle (although you are more than welcome to join me!). Rather, I hope that you come to understand that the principles and practice of living with less are pathways to liberation. That minimalism is a tool for self-discovery, allowing you to reveal more of yourself as you continue to grow and make space for the person you are meant to be. It is my hope that this journey liberates you to transform not only your home but your mindset as you choose to live with intention.

Whether you are a dear member of the AfroMini online community or have come across my unconventional guidance by happenstance, I want to thank you for being open to learning about a different approach to minimalism, one that is absent of rules regarding how many items you can own and what color your belongings have to be, and encourages authenticity over aesthetics.

Although you may be tempted to immediately begin the process of letting go, I recommend that you start with understanding the principles of minimalism, which are designed to prepare you for the physical and emotional labor ahead. This includes understanding the psychology of ownership and discovering the root causes of why you have more than you need. These principles will be essential to cultivate and maintain your lifestyle of living with less.

After understanding the principles of minimalism, the physical work of your journey will begin with a four-step process designed to help you let go of anything that no longer serves you. This includes (1) acknowledging that you have too much, (2) learning how to forgive yourself, (3) approaching letting go holistically, and (4) paying it forward with any items that can be used to assist others in need. Then, with helpful guidance, you will continue the beautiful work of defining your minimalist practice and continue the journey of living with less . . . *your way.*

Afrominimalism is my curated lifestyle of less, one that is informed by the history, culture, and beauty of the African diaspora. And it is no secret that this is an extension of my life's work. From my children's literature to my Afrocentric décor and wardrobe, I am proud to honor the cultural legacies of my people. As such, I would be remiss to not address my community directly in this text.

People of the African diaspora have a history of and continue to endure systematic oppression both domestically and abroad. Additionally, many of our inherited beliefs and habits have a profound influence on our relationship with money and ownership. The *State of Working America*, the Economic Policy Institute's flagship publication, highlights several startling statistics, such as the uncomfortable truth that Black Americans spend 4 percent more money annually than any other race despite the fact that they (1) are the least represented race and (2) live in poverty at the highest rate.[1] Even though Black Americans are the least represented and economically served population, as consumers they command $1.3 trillion in annual buying power.[2] We have significant power as one of the largest communities of consumers, yet our unique experiences are rarely addressed in the predominately White wellness and lifestyle industries.

As someone who struggled with the rigidity and complexity of mainstream minimalism, I now understand that this was largely due to the way representations of this lifestyle fail to include marginalized communities. I believe this shortcoming directly contributes to our community's reluctance to embrace the opportunities minimalism offers. Although the institution of slavery and legalized oppression after its abolition are significant contributing factors to the wealth gap, there is another rarely acknowledged contributing factor: choice. That is, the choice of where, how, and on what we choose to spend our dollars as well as to save and invest our resources to build generational wealth. But we have the power to change our narratives—for ourselves, our descendants, and the world in which we all inhabit.

Family and culture are the primary purchase influencers among Black consumers.[3] Therefore, throughout this guide are callouts labeled "For the Culture" that will address the specific needs and concerns of Black people and be relatable to other marginalized communities. For Black people, this information will highlight the impact of our history and culture, and how it relates to Black consumerism. Others should use these facts to gain awareness, build empathy, and, hopefully, identify ways to help course correct generational inequities.

Yes, this is a book about minimalism. But if we go beyond the surface of the aesthetics and delve into understanding the practice, conversations around spending and wealth are obvious points of discussion. Our individual, familial, and societal histories have collectively influenced our current culture of consumerism.

Again, I welcome you to this journey—*your* journey. You will experience many emotions, including laughter, frustration, and tears. And do not be surprised if you even express a few expletives along the way! It goes without saying that I believe every challenge you encounter (and conquer!) will be worth it. If you stay the course, I can assure you that learning to live with less will be one of the most liberating, transformative experiences you will have in this lifetime.

Thank you for being here.

Thank yourself for being here.

And welcome to *The Afrominimalist's Guide to Living with Less.*

meet your guide

THE AFROMINIMALIST

One of my greatest joys is being a storyteller and so, if you'll indulge me, I'd like to tell you a story:

When I resigned from my appointment as a senior policy advisor with the U.S. Department of Energy in October 2015, it was a pivotal moment in my professional career, but I had no idea that it would be a defining moment in my personal life as well. I only knew that the time had come for me to leave my "good government job," and there was little anyone could say to convince me otherwise. I feared that if I stayed in the role just for the cushy salary and benefits, I would never do the work I felt called to do—preserve and celebrate the history and culture of the African diaspora.

Before receiving my juris doctor in 2006, I earned undergraduate and graduate degrees in African and African-American studies.

Although today these qualifications are respected and in demand, the world was different a mere two decades ago. There weren't many viable professions devoted to the study of Black lives outside of academia and becoming a tenured professor didn't interest me at the time. Still, I needed a livelihood. And I needed it sooner rather than later. I had given birth to my only child while in law school, my beautiful daughter, Nalah, and the added pressures of single motherhood only made success seem more urgent.

I had always been determined. I mean, I was the woman who sat on a medical cushion at the beginning of her second year of law school rather than let recent childbirth force her to defer the entire semester. Pursuing a nontraditional career for my discipline seemed an easy quest. But after being unemployed for several months after graduating law school, my steadfast faith and fortitude began to waver.

When a career counselor recommended that I change my resume to reflect that my academic disciplines were in the social sciences instead of Black studies so employers could focus more on my law degree, I was hesitant. Although these were seemingly small changes, they felt deceitful, if not to employers, then surely to me. Despite the low marketability and job prospects, I had majored in Black studies (and defended my decision) because learning the history of the African diaspora awakened a sense of purpose and being. It was what I loved! But I also loved my daughter and wanted to provide her with stability. Begrudgingly, I revised my resume, and within a month, I received my first job offer from a boutique law firm that focused on environmental justice—I'd be able to utilize my Black studies degrees after all.

Energy and environmental law were still developing sectors,

and terms like "renewables" and "sustainability" had yet to become mainstream. However, within a few short years, energy efficiency was at the forefront of climate change and I found myself as one of the few Black women in a booming industry. That meant I could write my own ticket. And I did!

I transitioned from more meaningful plaintiffs' work into Big Law, where I spent my days and nights supporting demanding partners with million-dollar transactions for wind turbine development, credit swap agreements, and other lucrative project finance deals. In exchange for a higher salary, I was required to meet strict billable hour requirements—a minimum of 2,100 hours a year. Long days and nights became the norm. On the weekends, my toddler often joined me in the office, setting up shop under my desk, where she found joy coloring and watching DVDs. Of course, I felt like the worst mother in the world.

The more hours I worked, the more I earned, and found myself hating the career I once coveted. And I began to seek solace through emotional spending. E-commerce was also a rapidly developing sector, and in addition to shopping in brick-and-mortar stores, I enjoyed the ease and convenience of making online purchases to mask my unhappiness. Every pay period I treated myself, my daughter, and sometimes even family and friends to the latest and greatest indulgences. My rationale was we had earned it—me by working twelve-plus-hour days, my daughter by having to deal with always being the last child to get picked up from day care, and my loved ones by tolerating my hectic schedule and unavailability.

Even though I knew Big Law was an unsustainable way of life for a single mother, I was determined to sustain it for as long as possible. The money was good, and the perks were great (whenever I had time to use the discounted membership at the luxury gym across the street from the law firm). Having the financial means to buy whatever I wanted felt like a dream (even though my work-life balance was a nightmare).

Although I spent a lot of my disposable income, by 2008 I managed to save enough to purchase my first property: a 630-square-foot, one-bed, one-bath condo with a den for me and my toddler, the cutest spot that I could find in a major metropolitan city. It was a small home, but it was ours. And I enjoyed decorating it lavishly, filling every nook and cranny with high-end furnishings. Single motherhood was hard. If I was going to be in struggle mode 24/7, the least I could do was surround myself with beautiful things.

Thankfully, I did not have to go it alone for long. In 2010, at an after-work March Madness gathering, I met the man who would ultimately become my husband. Less than a year later, we were married, both of us wide-eyed, first-time six-figure income earners who knew little more to do with our combined wages than spend them.

And spend we did.

Rather than begin our new marital life in my small but affordable condo, we purchased a 2,500-square-foot home and blissfully began doing what we'd always been forewarned *not* to do: trying to keep up with the Joneses. Hell, we *were* the Joneses! We drove luxury cars, enjoyed date nights at the finest restaurants, and wore the labels of high-end designers. Weekdays were meant for working. Weekends were meant for indulging.

But even with a partner, work-life balance in Big Law remained impossible. Just when I felt as though I could no longer manage the stress of billable hour requirements, something miraculous happened: Barack Obama was elected the forty-fourth president of the United States. I saw no greater opportunity than serving under his administration and I transitioned from the private sector to government in 2010. I was over the billable hour requirement, over my work serving private organizations rather than underserved populations, so when I was hired to serve as a senior policy advisor at the U.S. Department of Energy, I thought I had finally found my golden ticket. But in time, this role also lost its appeal. That was why it was also not so difficult to leave that six-figure job five years later.

After spending more than ten years working in a profession that paid well but did little to bring me personal fulfillment, I wanted to pursue what I loved. I had recently rediscovered my passion for storytelling, a favorite pastime from my adolescence. As an adult, I realized it was the perfect way to merge everything that I loved: research, writing, and teaching the history and culture of the African diaspora. Becoming an author of historical fiction and fantasy seemed in divine alignment with the next chapter of my life, and I could not wait to spend my days getting rich while living out my purpose. (I held on to this dream regardless of the numerous articles written by actual authors who stated in very plain terms that one wrote for the love of writing, not for wealth, because there are few professions that are more unpredictable.)

After independently publishing my novel, *The Truth About Awiti*, its surprise success led to me acquiring literary representation. Although it is embarrassing to admit now, I was certain I was about to become the next great American novelist. So, even though our family had little savings, I had few worries. Besides, I had a husband with a stable career—a security blanket that made leaving my own livelihood more comforting.

During the first few months of being a full-time creative, I basked in my newfound freedom from the daily commute and nine-to-five grind. I pivoted quickly, shifting my focus from reviewing contracts to spending my days writing historical fiction. I spent my mornings and afternoons in coffee shops, another fulfilled aspect of the writer's life I'd romanticized until I realized it was much easier (and cheaper) to make coffee at home. In the evenings, I was determined to be a fully present mother and wife.

I failed miserably at all of it.

After years of conditioning to account for my time in six-minute increments, I found it incredibly frustrating that creativity refused to adhere to my carefully structured schedule. Moreover, my family had new expectations now that I was "home all day." I began to resent those evenings when my creativity had just started flowing only to have to forgo my attempts at storytelling to transition to the demands of being a homemaker.

But something else troubled me, an uncomfortable truth that became more unavoidable as the months progressed. Home alone for the majority of the day, I was up close and personal with just how much house and how much stuff our family had. Even worse, I noticed seemingly for the first time how much of our space and things we did not need and were not using. The harshest of this reality? Knowing that I was responsible for the bulk of what we owned.

My husband's wardrobe had long-since been relegated to the

closet in his home office (thanks to my shopping hobby). I needed to utilize both closets in our bedroom (in addition to the closet in our guest bedroom!) to hold all my clothing, shoes, and accessories. My then-preteen daughter's room was filled with more stuffed animals and toys than she could ever play with, as well as miniature furnishings and playthings to ensure her American Girl doll's life perfectly mirrored her own. Whenever I cleaned her room, I could not help but associate many of her belongings with former Big Law projects—the result of gifts I had given her because I felt guilty for working such long hours.

Everywhere I looked, there was evidence of my years of emotional spending and bargain shopping. There were things left over from my former corporate and government careers. Things that I believed a wealthy Black family living in the suburbs of DC should own. Things that I had acquired simply because a little red sticker told me that I was getting a deal. So. Many. Things. The majority of which none of us needed, used, or loved.

Less than a year into pursuing my dream of becoming the next great American novelist, as I struggled to write and found myself frequently distracted by our clutter, the moment came when I decided I had enough, both literally and figuratively. Little did I know that this feeling of "enough" was my first step to learning to live with authenticity and intention. I was tapping into my superpowers, but I had no idea that to fully harness their potential, I would first have to learn a few valuable lessons: why I had more than I needed and why it was so hard to let go of things that no longer served me. I would have to learn more about the word that always appeared whenever I desperately searched for ways to simplify my life: "minimalism."

The Journey Begins

I still remember that Saturday morning in June, a beautiful warm day that beckoned me to spend time outdoors. But instead of making plans to enjoy the idyllic weather, I was preparing to spend the weekend like I had spent so many others before: cleaning. Now hyper-aware of our excess, I had also planned to sort  through our belongings to see what could be donated. But just the mere thought of the tasks ahead made me anxious.

There was just so much stuff! Our wardrobes were overflowing with clothing, shoes, and accessories. Every room contained unnecessary home goods, tarnishing trinkets, and dusty candles with unlit wicks. Less than two hours into the endeavor, I was exasperated. Rather than spend more time trying to sort through our belongings, I decided it would be easier to purchase more storage solutions to keep everything out of sight. Pacing through the house, hopeful to find places to put additional decorative bins and baskets, I paused.

Was I really about to buy more stuff to hide the stuff that I had?

Nah. It was time for a change. It was time for *me* to change. And living with less seemed to be the only solution. So, I decided to dig a little deeper into understanding what it meant to embrace the practice of minimalism.

At first, I was intrigued by the concept of living with so few things. Then I became enchanted with minimalists' personal stories, fascinated by their chronicles of obtaining freedom and autonomy through the simple act of letting go of what no longer served them. Soon I had developed a full-on obsession with small-space living. Image after image, blog post after blog post, I gathered intel from strangers who it seemed had mastered the art of living with less.

I envied the large, barren residences tastefully decorated in neutrals and the tiny houses that managed to contain everything one needed in less square footage than our kitchen. Minimalist dwellings managed to strike a balance that I did not even know was possible, somehow appearing both sterile yet serene. Everything looked so clean! Everyone looked so happy!

"That's it," I declared. "I'm done with all this stuff. I am going to be a minimalist."

There was no need to make a list of pros and cons to aid in my decision making. No need to discuss and seek approval from family and friends. That was how certain I was that living with less was the answer to all my problems.

Life sure looked simpler without all the excess.

Convinced that adopting a minimalist lifestyle was the only sure pathway to escape my overconsumption, I changed my search terms from "minimalism" to "how to become a minimalist." But instead of finding information on how to make a seamless transition to moderation, there were just more pictures of minimalist décor and personal success stories. To make matters worse, there was little commonality between the latter. If one person declared that a minimalist had to own one hundred items or less, another proclaimed that counting one's belongings was unnecessary and instead offered solutions on how to create a minimalist aesthetic. Everyone seemed to be an unofficial authority on the subject, offering photographic evidence of their tidy spaces and smiling faces as proof they were doing it right.

The more I tried to learn about how to become a minimalist, the more frustrated I became. For a practice that was supposed to encourage simplicity, minimalism was becoming more complicated by the minute.

How many items could I own *exactly*? Did I have to replace our home's colorful, cheerful interior with boring shades of beige? Did I need to throw away *all* of my home goods? Even the ones that held cultural significance? And what about my books? How was I supposed to own less than a hundred items *and* keep my beloved collection of literary fiction and historical texts?!

Searching for guidance on how to pare down my attire was not much easier. Every capsule wardrobe collection looked the same—relatively empty closets with a few clothing options that could be mixed and matched to maximize versatility. Even though I rarely wore any of my designer clothing and accessories as a stay-at-home-wife-mother-creative, I cringed at the thought of getting rid of my beautiful timeless pieces in exchange for black-and-white "investment pieces." Surely I would not miss wearing colorful patterns and prints when I could just embrace a modest, colorless uniform . . . every single day . . . for the rest of my life . . . right? *Right?*

Doubts abounded, but I was so convinced that if I could just pare down a little more, really, truly simplify, I would achieve the bliss I saw online. If I could just find a pair of shoes that worked for all reasons and seasons, I'd be set!

Honestly, it was much easier to just *look* at the lives of minimalists, to daydream about the life of simplicity that I wanted.

But soon, that, too, presented its own challenges. Although minimalist homes and capsule collections were beautifully understated, whenever I checked the price tags to see if my dreams were within reach, I realized simplicity was *expensive*! I began to wonder if I was even in the right tax bracket to make such a dramatic lifestyle change.

The more I tried to figure out how I would whittle down our seemingly tens of thousands of things to a mere one hundred items, the more impossible it all seemed. But if I wanted to happily live with less, what other choice did I have but to try? Besides, I would only need to dedicate a weekend to change our lives for the better. There were enough minimalists who declared decluttering a "weekend warrior" mission for me to believe it was true. Two days of sorting through all our stuff to discover what sparked joy seemed like a small sacrifice to gain a lifetime of simplicity.

And so, it began.

And Then, Divorce

As the months passed, I dedicated more time to minimalism than I did trying to become a novelist. After a major publisher rejected my second attempt at writing historical fiction, my belief in my ability to be a writer took a devastating blow. Sorting through unwanted clothing and home goods was daunting, but it was less painful than staring at a blank piece of paper with a pen in my hand for hours on end. The process of decluttering was slow, but at least I was making progress doing something.

My daughter's private school tuition became harder to pay. Credit card bills and installment loans started to lapse. Our finances grew tighter, and well, there's no problems like money problems. My husband and I were both at our wits' end. Less than one year after my bold (and very public) declaration on social media to resign from the grind to #dowhatyoulove, I was finally willing to accept defeat. Just as quickly as it had joyfully begun, our façade of being "the Joneses" had ended.

Although my decision to leave my good government job was not the only reason our marriage became increasingly stressful, it was without a doubt a contributing factor. We had known each other less than a year before we got married, hardly enough time to develop a friendship. There had certainly been more good times than bad, which made it easy to mask any unhappiness and unfulfillment during our seasons of plenty. But in the midst of our first major crisis, a toxic mixture of mounting debt, job insecurity, and uncertainty, the reality that we were strangers in our union was hard to ignore. Soon it became clear that my dream of being the next great American novelist wasn't the only thing that was over. Our six-year marriage would end in divorce. And I had no clue how I would survive the fall.

The decision to file to end our union was ultimately mine, so it was hard for me not to take the lion's share of the blame. What if I had made better choices? What if instead of purchasing stuff with our disposable income, I had saved? What if I had not romanticized the idea of being a full-time writer, which added the extra pressure of living on one income?

What if? What if? *What if!*

Even though our divorce was amicable—a true conscious uncoupling that made it easier on our family and friends—it was still a difficult time. Separating two lives that been intended to be one forevermore was complicated. Of course, there was our joint debt and all the things to divvy up. But the biggest consideration was housing.

Already stretched to the limit with my own mortgage and student loans as well as personal and credit card debt when we married, our marital property was solely in my husband's name. During our marriage, I had rented out my condo and enjoyed spending most of the profit I earned. Without employment, my options for housing during our separation (a requirement for our divorce to be granted!) were limited. In fact, I only had one option—giving my tenant notice so I could return to reside in my affordable little condo.

I never imagined I would have to return to where I started, especially with less than what I had.

When I entered my old-new home, the space felt smaller than I remembered. The tiny den-turned-bedroom that had been perfect for my toddler now seemed an impractical space for a pre-teen. A mere ten paces down the hall was my bedroom, which was decent in size but still a reflection of the compromises that come with city living. There were none of the conveniences like a walk-in closet or private bathroom. Even worse, the walls were still painted a warm, sunny yellow—a color that did everything but make me feel joyful.

Always kind and willing to do whatever he could to mitigate our unfortunate circumstances, my soon-to-be ex-husband took on the responsibility of continuing to tackle our joint debt. With only monthly child support and a small savings, there would be no hiring of contractors to help manage the upgrades the condo so desperately needed. Still beholden to the mainstream minimalist aesthetic I had come to admire, I chose to refresh the walls in "New Home White" and repainted the entire condo myself, buying one gallon of paint at a time. Thankfully, the color made the space feel newer and representative of a fresh start.

Without enough funds to decorate and furnish the entire condo, I made the motherly sacrifice of taking care of my daughter's bedroom first. The first night together at our old-new home, she slept peacefully on her new IKEA daybed, her young mind finally at ease in a familiar space. I lay awake for hours, my mattress on the floor as I stared at small slivers of yellow paint around the windowsills in my bedroom, evidence of where I had run out of paint and the budget to buy more.

Seemingly overnight, my journey to minimalism had quickly gone from a conscious choice to circumstantial. Despite knowing my situation was temporary, it felt very permanent and embarrassingly so. The year before, I could buy whatever I wanted and now, I could barely afford and had to ration cans of paint! I could not help but see myself as the protagonist in an ever-developing tragic comedy—the woman with advanced degrees, unemployed with an empty bank account but a closet filled with designer clothing, shoes, and handbags.

I had come across a profound Cree Native American proverb while conducting research for *The Truth About Awiti*:

"Only when the last tree has been cut down, the last fish been caught, and the last stream poisoned, will we realize we cannot eat money."

And I could not help but feel the same way about my dire situation. Sometimes I would look in my closet in shame and say aloud, "You can't eat handbags, Christine."

Days were a blur of dropping my daughter off at school and returning home to search for employment. During those times I could not bear to read another thank-you-for-your-application-you-are-highly-qualified-but-we-selected-another-candidate letter, I lay in bed and worried how long it would be until I felt stable again.

Every night, I promised myself that as soon as I was on the other side of this seemingly insurmountable mountain of hardship, I would make better choices. I promised myself, I would never be in such a situation by my own doing ever again.

A New Beginning

"Just keep living."

One of my favorite Black folks' adages is "Just keep living," which is another way of saying, "This, too, shall pass." And even though some days were significantly harder than others, that is exactly what I did. I kept living. Which most days seemed to be the only thing I *could* do.

Despite the embarrassment, there was an unexpected power in acknowledging my role in the decisions and choices that led to my financial difficulties. I spent time reading about the triggers of emotional spending and learning about what it meant to be a conscious consumer. Rather than make plans for what I would buy with my first paycheck, I created a spreadsheet for the bills I would pay off first. Always one to avoid answering 1-800 numbers that I knew were creditors seeking payment, I boldly faced my debt by calling lenders first. After humbly (and humiliatingly) explaining my circumstances, I set up forbearances, deferments, and payment plans.

I was growing. Even though it was slow and painful at times, it was growth. And every little milestone made me proud of the decisions I was making to regain control of my life.

As I kept living, I kept searching for employment. I updated my resume to honestly note my desire to utilize my Black studies degrees. Each rejection hit hard but only made me more determined. Then in late 2017, I was approached with a seemingly perfect opportunity to manage a new university center, the first of its kind, and one that combined my experience in policy, advocacy, and the preservation of Black lives: managing director of the Antiracist Research & Policy Center at American University.

Finally, I was employed! Bills were paid down. And then, paid off. Soon I had savings again, a feat I thought it would take a lifetime to achieve. I had survived the unthinkable. My season of hardship had ended and life felt like a new beginning.

After emerging from such a long period of scarcity, the old me would have indulged, first by decorating our old-new space quickly. Next, I would have purchased the latest gadgets for my teen and splurged on some high-end fashion for myself. What better way to prove to everyone who had been watching my shit show that I stepped into the next chapter of my life stronger and better than ever?

But the new me remembered how suddenly life can change, and how awful it was to be unprepared for the expected. "Remember, you can't eat handbags, Christine." So, I decided to adhere to the advice from a small community of minimalists I had recently begun to follow on social media. Rather than buy all the things I wanted and *thought* I needed, I decided to live in the small space for a while to see what I *actually* needed.

It was my first time exercising a new muscle, one that I would need to develop and use repeatedly on my journey to minimalism: restraint.

Even though my decision was wise, it wasn't easy. Living in our simply furnished, undecorated condo often made me feel uneasy, and I struggled with feelings of inadequacy. Even though I knew having a home filled with things did not mean stability and guarantee happiness, it was still hard to shake the ideals that such a life represented. I argued with the voice in my head trying to shame me for being an adult without a couch and coffee table with matching side tables in her living room. *The horror!*

Only my closest friends were welcome visitors, the handful of trusted confidants who had supported me through the divorce and its tumultuous aftermath. They had already seen and loved me through my worst, so they knew my new lifestyle was progressing toward becoming my best.

Whenever I felt especially tempted, I turned to my new minimalist online community for support and encouragement. Although most were living with less by choice, there were some people who had also become minimalists by circumstance. We bonded over the irony of formerly having everything we wanted yet feeling empty and the important lessons we'd recently learned.

Despite the challenges, we agreed that our lives were much better even though we had less.

We were growing, and it felt good not to have to go it alone.

Becoming the Afrominimalist

Little by little, I began buying things our home needed. But after a brief flirtation with the neutral minimalist décor that called me to the practice, I realized I was doing the exact opposite of what the lifestyle encouraged—being intentional. My home didn't feel . . . well, like *home*. And I couldn't figure out why. I mean, every room was spotless, every space as hygge as possible. So why didn't I feel the sense of joy and freedom that so many minimalists had promised?

It took some time to realize that my discontent was caused by the fact that, although I was living with less, the décor that I'd chosen was a reflection of the minimalist aesthetics I'd come to admire. I missed welcoming, warm colors and textures in my living room. I wanted elements of cultural significance on display. And even though these essentials were a far cry from mainstream minimalism, I knew that what was missing in my home was authenticity, a reflection of who I am and what I value at my core.

So, I decided to do minimalism my way.

I began curating my wardrobe and home with colorful Ankara prints, playful textiles, and mud cloth—purposeful, intentional décor that made me happy. My favorite keepsake is a jar of raw cotton that reminds me to thank and honor my ancestors daily, and which also served as inspiration for this guide. Filling my living space with only the things I needed, used, and loved resulted in my own style of minimalism, one that is authentic and aligned with my passion and purpose: Afrominimalism.[1]

As popularity and curiosity about living with less continued to gain momentum, the small online community I cherished grew to a large, varied group of people who were committed to practicing minimalism their way, too! There were families who lived in campers and converted school buses. Empty-nesters residing in refurbished Airstreams. Newlyweds who were also new tiny-home enthusiasts.

I continued to chronicle my journey online just in case there was anyone else looking for inspiration or a different approach to living with less. Especially Black people. I knew that some of my former excess had been the result of trying to flex by living up to cultural expectations, of trying to "keep up with the Joneses." I wanted other Black professionals, especially first-generation college graduates and high-income earners, to liberate themselves, too! Afrominimalism became a platform to show my community what minimalism could look like "for the culture" and the many benefits it offers.

Joyfully, I used social media to give others a peek into my colorful, Afrocentric world. And I am sure that you can guess the handle that I chose: @Afrominimalist.

Today, I own less than I ever thought possible, but my life feels more abundant with everything! Time. Resources. Joy. Peace. Less of what I do not need. More of what I love. I let go of a lot, but I kept what mattered most.

In addition to helping rid my life of excess, minimalism also empowered me to embrace a radical reimagining of home as a sanctuary. A place to unplug, rest, recharge, recenter, and recommit to my priorities and purpose. Each room reflects and represents my life, and I remain intentional to ensure that my home only contains things that are necessary to sustain and bring me joy. Scents that are uplifting. Colors that calm or motivate. Clothing that flatters my body type and embodies my personality. Objects and trinkets that remind me of who I am, what my ancestors overcame, and what I want loved ones to inherit. This process of self-discovery expanded beyond my home and wardrobe as I learned to be intentional and authentic in every aspect of my being. And I want this same liberation and reimagining for you.

So now, let us begin your journey with the understanding that the only destination is the ever-moving target of becoming the best version of yourself. I am honored to serve as a guide to embracing the practice of minimalism. Your way.

part one

THE PRINCIPLES

minimalism

AN INTRODUCTION

Although its origins are rooted in artistic design and expression, today minimalism is best known as a lifestyle trend that encourages simplicity. These days we talk about our homes, décor, productivity, wardrobes, and even our digital spaces as opportunities to practice minimalism. Regardless of the subject, the principles of the practice are intended to achieve a desired result: minimizing excess to ensure life is filled with only what matters.

But because the word "minimalism" has become almost synonymous with clean lines and a neutral, simplistic aesthetic, many people believe (incorrectly) that there is only one way minimalism can look. So, let's get one thing straight: Minimalism is a practice. It is a mindset. A choice. A lifestyle. And *so* much more than an aesthetic. You do not need to commit yourself to

Scandinavian furniture and white walls in order to commit to the practice of living with less.

In its simplest form, minimalism requires you to be authentic and intentional about what you choose to keep and what you allow into your life. The "keep" part of the equation is often the focus of documentaries and other media, amplified by people gathering and sorting through their belongings to find what "sparks joy." Deciding what to keep is, indeed, important (and we'll talk more about that in Part Two, "The Process"), but it's not the whole story. How and why people acquire so many things, why we allow what we do into our lives is an aspect that is less commonly addressed. Instead, many practitioners create confusing rules and guidelines to prevent acquisitions, often setting expectations that seem unrealistic for the average person.

Good news: If these unofficial policies about minimalism seem unrealistic to you, it's because they are! In fact, trying to conform your home, wardrobe, and other personal aspects of your life to mirror someone else's is the antithesis of the practice. If the mindset of a minimalist is grounded in authenticity and intentionality, then your own lived experience of minimalism should be as varied and unique as we are. That is why I encourage anyone who wants to live with less to focus on authenticity over aesthetics.

We Are All Consumers

"We are all consumers, people who purchase and acquire goods for personal use. Our choices impact not only our own lives but also extend to the mak-

ers of these goods and their impact on the environment. The minimalist mindset is one of conscious
consumerism."

—Christine

As a lifestyle, minimalism means making a commitment
to be a more conscious consumer. This act of intention
requires you to move responsibly as you decide what to
keep and allow into your life. This includes being honest
about your needs and what makes you happy, and edu-
cating yourself about the true cost of your purchases beyond their price tags. To be a conscious consumer, you
must be aware of how your choices impact not only your
lifestyle and finances but the laborers producing these
goods, as well as their environmental footprint. Our
spending affects more than our wallets and what we acquire in our homes. Minimalism is an opportunity for us
to be intentional in our consumption.

Just as my journey led me to a style that I like to call Afrominimalism, your journey will lead you to your own personal style.
And keep in mind that it may even change over time.

Your journey to become a minimalist is a process of self-
discovery that will not happen overnight. So, remember to be
patient and don't rush to conform to an aesthetic that you *think*
minimalism *should* look like. As you embrace the principles and
practice of living with less, allow authenticity to be your guide.
Your home décor, wardrobe, and other personal effects should be

representative of your core values, but what values you choose and how you choose to reflect these areas of importance may take time. Despite the temptation of commodified simplicity, being authentic in your approach to minimalism is the only sure way to successfully embrace and maintain your new lifestyle. We have to start with ourselves.

why you have more
than you need

I still remember the large piles of clothing sitting atop my bed. The numerous shoes and accessories scattered across the floor. And me, standing in the middle of the chaos, overwhelmed and sobbing, "I can't believe I have all this stuff!" It didn't help to know that I still had several more closets, bins, and baskets to conquer. It was such a sobering reality as I began my journey to live with less. There was no way to deny it any longer: I had more than I needed.

A recent article in the *Los Angeles Times* noted that the average American household has more than 300,000 items,[1] a staggering statistic given that these families have fewer than three individuals.[2] And although children in the United States account for 3.7 percent of the world's youth, they are the recipients of 47 percent of all toys and children's books.[3] More people use their two-car garages for storage than to park their two cars. Let's face it: Most of us have a lot of stuff.

There are so many reasons we have more than we need. But often, even as we stare at piles of our belongings, trying to account for *how*—the shopping sprees, tiny indulgences accumulated over the years, the gifts we received—we still don't really understand *why*. Which is exactly why this is where your journey to minimalism will start: by first identifying and understanding the reasons underlying why you have accumulated so much. Unless we understand the root causes of our overconsumption, we risk finding ourselves in the same situation time and time again.

Identifying why you have more than you need requires a bit of inner work. One of the first assessments is understanding the difference between our necessities and wants, because, believe it or not, many people blur the line between the two to justify their spending behaviors. I know I sure did!

From owning excessive amounts of clothing to purchasing more food than we can consume, our decisions to purchase things are often rooted in our belief that we *need* them. We need work attire and evening wear for black-tie affairs. We need to make sure our kitchens and freezers are well-stocked with staples and nonperishables in case of an emergency. But do we need as much as we acquire? Usually, no. That is why we must make the connection between how our desire to have our needs met often results in excess.

Through my own experiences as well as speaking with countless individuals about their journeys to minimalism, I identified four common threads that often influence our spending hab-its. Keep in mind this is not an inclusive list of all the reasons for our overconsumption, but they are among the most preva-lent. Many of our habits and behaviors are extensions of our childhood experiences. Others are the results of cultural and societal pressures and expectations, trying to "keep up with the Joneses," or mindless consumption. Regardless, the end result is the same: These factors and others contribute to us having more than we need.

It Started in Childhood

You might be surprised to know that the most difficult part of my journey was not the physical process of letting go of items that I did not need or use. Yes, decluttering was daunting and over-whelming, but owning up to the truth that I had so many things was hardest to accept. I discovered so many items with price tags still attached, it was beyond shameful. But they held one of the clues behind my why: Most, if not all, of the tags were red.

Markdowns. Price cuts. Sale stickers on top of sale stickers to denote just how much of a deal I was getting. I had plenty of evidence that I was a bargain shopper. But it took a lot of soul searching for me to realize that I was in love with the thrill of the hunt and less enthused with the prize.

Sales provided an instant rush of dopamine. Whenever I found a discounted item, I became excited with the idea of get-ting a bargain and usually purchased it. Besides, I had to get the deal before someone else did. From getting up early to wait in line on Black Fridays to considering whether I should petition to make bargain shopping an Olympic sport, I loved, seriously *loved* scoring a deal. Whenever I had free time on the weekends, more than likely I was in pursuit of the next great find.

That day I stood crying as I stared at piles of my belongings, I knew many of the items were the result of my emotionally driven shopping sprees. But I also knew there had to be more to it. Why did I resort to shopping in times of distress? Why did I find hunting for a deal more therapeutic than, say, going for a run or seeking solace on my yoga mat? Why did I find joy in scoring a bargain, but then never or rarely used the items once I brought them home? As I asked myself these questions, I thought back to when my shopping habits first began. I realized that shopping for leisure instead of a purpose started in my childhood.

Some of my fondest memories are going on weekend shopping excursions with my mother. We frequented department stores and thrift stores, and there was nothing like finding something so discounted it would be criminal to leave it behind. For my mother, it was a way to decompress from a stressful workweek. But for me, these experiences became associated with having fun.

Weekends were our special mother-daughter time. We made trips to the mall during the best of times or to our local thrift stores when money was tight. No matter my mother's financial situation, the day always ended with ice cream—mint chocolate chip or rainbow sherbet for me and rum raisin for her. When we returned home, my mother was happy and relaxed. And I was a sticky, joyful, and satisfied mess, already counting down the days until our next weekend adventure.

In high school, I took on my first job as a salesclerk at a trendy retail store called Merry-Go-Round. In addition to being able to purchase the latest fashions with my generous employee discount, I was able to use this incentive at several other retail divisions. Every payday, most of my earnings usually went right back to my employer—the beginnings of my choice to seek personal fulfilment and enjoyment by getting a deal.

This behavior continued throughout my young adult years, and when I went to college, I obtained my first credit cards. Every Wednesday, creditors set up their promotional tables near the library or dining halls—locations where they knew cash-strapped students would find the allure of possibly getting a credit card *and* a free gift for completing the application irresistible. So many free T-shirts and water bottles! So much excitement when the envelope containing plastic money arrived in the mail! So many purchases of twenty-five-cent wings . . . with interest! Of course, such behavior is deemed predatory now. But I am among countless individuals who spent much of their adult years trying to rebuild their credit history after buying things on credit as a broke college student.

When I became an adult, shopping continued to be a way to lift my spirits whenever I felt down. It was a way to reward myself whenever I felt that I had worked too much. A way to pass the time when I was bored or uninspired. A way to feel proud of my accomplishments as I adorned myself in beautiful professional attire and decorated my home with furnishings that represented my success.

The emotional connection I had to shopping as a source of enjoyment and relaxation began decades ago, on those weekends where I spent the day bargain hunting with my first best friend—my mother. Even as an adult, it is not uncommon for me to end a shopping spree with eating mint chocolate chip ice cream.

So much of who we are and how we behave or respond to certain situations is rooted in our childhood. Whether it's always looking for a deal, our innate response to stock our pantries because we grew up with food scarcity, or even conforming to gender roles, the behaviors and experiences from our childhood often inform our adult spending habits. What we watched, were told, and learned from our caregivers and community often have a profound impact on our relationship with money and how we spend it.

Often, we are unaware of how these experiences impact our lives on even the smallest levels. One of the stories I like to share that underscores just how deeply our childhood influences our adult behaviors involves one of my friends and her dear husband, who has an affinity for using a lot of dish soap when he washes the dishes. To protect their identity, even though there is no shame in any of our childhood stories—we did not *choose* our caregivers—let's call this wonderful couple Mary and Brian.

One day, as Mary and I engaged in conversation about the husbands we loved but who annoyed us so much, she shared, "I just walked past the kitchen and Brian is in there washing dishes. Girl, the bubbles are literally overflowing out of the sink! I just don't know why he has to use so much dish soap and make such a mess!"

Ever the friend who equally complained about such trivial matters, I laughed. "Well, at least he's doing the dishes!"

"Seriously," Mary said. "He's been doing this ever since we got married. It's so annoying and unnecessary."

Upon realizing this was a true sore spot for her, I inquired, "Well, have you ever asked him why he does that?"

A few days later, she told me that she did indeed ask Brian about his obsession with dish soap bubbles and was moved to discover why. Although he was now successful and quite wealthy, Brian had grown up poor. Raised by his grandmother in the Deep South, most of their household items were purchased at dollar stores and, even then, had to be used in moderation. Whenever Brian washed the dishes, his grandmother only let him use minuscule amounts of dish soap, just enough to clean the dishes and never enough to make bubbles. So, now that he is an adult, he buys the best dish soap and enjoys making as many bubbles as he wants. Where my friend Mary sees a mess, Brian finds fulfillment in bubbles overflowing out of the sink, and enjoys an experience he longed for but never got to delight in as a child.

As you begin the self-discovery of learning about why you have more than you need, think about how your childhood experiences may have knowingly or unknowingly influenced your behaviors. Think about what your caregivers determined were necessities and how they went about both acquiring and managing them. Consider how they prioritized their spending to meet your family's needs versus fulfilling their personal wants. Reflect on how your circumstances with abundance or scarcity may be influencing your current decisions.

Ask Yourself

What Did I Learn About Spending and Saving as a Child?

1. Was money—spending and saving—talked about openly in your home? If so, was the discussion healthy or a source of contention?
2. Did you receive an allowance? If so, did you have to "earn it" or was it given freely?
3. How did your family celebrate milestones and key achievements? Were you rewarded with money, gifts, or nontangible affirmations?
4. What did your family do for fun? Which experiences were considered regular activities, and which were considered "a treat"?
5. Can you identify unmet needs and desires from your childhood? If so, how have they shown up in adulthood and/or in what ways do you find yourself seeking to resolve them?

Take a moment to reflect on your answers to these questions. Consider writing your answers in a journal and take note, also, of any memories that surface, stories you heard growing up, or events that seem particularly significant. Your answers to these questions may come in handy during the "letting go" process, as part of the work involves acknowledging that you have more than you need.

As you are thinking through your past, remember to revisit these situations through the eyes of your younger self. When I answered these questions, I recalled my mother prioritized meeting our needs over her wants (which I sincerely appreciate!). Whenever she purchased something for herself during our weekend shopping sprees, it was always on sale and it was usually something small—a new lipstick or clothing and accessories that I now understand she needed for work.

Because money was rarely discussed in our household, I knew very little about the weighted financial responsibilities of adulthood. I mean, I knew that adults went to work and got paid for whatever they did. I knew that there were obviously some jobs that paid more than others based on what my friends had or didn't have. And I knew that parents held the purse strings, that because they earned the money, they also earned the right to determine how it was spent. But aside from these basic observations, money was "grown folks" business.

If I wanted something, I simply asked my mother and if she had the resources, the answer was "yes." But if she did not have them, the answer was "no." End of story.

Think About It

Consider *how* money and requests were addressed by your caregivers. Asking for an item and being told, "No, you don't need that right now," or, "Why don't you add that to your Christmas list" is very different from being ridiculed about your request or receiving an angry response akin to, "I told you to stop asking me for stuff! We don't have money to waste on foolishness!"

It may also be helpful to reflect on your family's history to gain a better understanding of how your *caregivers* developed their spending habits. My mother was born a little over a decade after the Great Depression, therefore her family surely experienced some of the financial hardships that impacted so many. Without a doubt, they experienced some form of food scarcity, because I was constantly reminded to "clean my plate" since it was important to not waste anything, especially food. Even now as an adult, I struggle with the idea of throwing away an unfinished meal. At restaurants, I always ask for a doggy bag and if something I despise, like tomatoes, is added to my order, I'd rather pick them out than send it back to the kitchen because I know that a perfectly good meal will be thrown in the garbage. And again, this is not because I *experienced* food scarcity as a child; this behavior is due to the guilt that was always *associated* with wasting food as a child.

The last consideration I want to address when it comes to understanding how childhood influences adult behaviors is the longing many people feel to satisfy unfulfilled childhood wants and needs. Whereas Brian's childhood longing resulted in the harmless accumulation of overflowing bubbles in the kitchen sink, the need to fulfill our childhood desires can result in more expensive indulgences. Many of us may remember saying, "I can't wait until I grow up, because when I do, I am going to do/buy whatever I want!" And most of us remain incredibly determined

FOR THE CULTURE

▼▲▼▲▼

Honestly, I do not even know where to begin with this one. Depending on your age, aspects of my personal story likely resonated with you directly. People who grew up during the 1970s and '80s lived with the constant guilt of waste, from being told to clean our plates because there were "starving children in Africa who would love to have our food" to being reminded that we were the first generation with a real chance to make something of ourselves so we better not waste the opportunities our ancestors died for, especially obtaining an education. Coupled with the generational trauma of systemic oppression that impacted our communities, Black Americans have a lot to reflect on when it comes to understanding how our childhoods impacted our spending habits. These are both familial and community considerations because many of us were truly raised by "a village" and, therefore, were influenced by our neighborhoods and churches as well. Consider doing this work with family members or friends to help you talk and work through understanding (and forgiving!) people who played a role in establishing your relationship with earning, saving, and spending money.

and have been successful in achieving this declaration. Often, fulfilling our unresolved childhood wants and needs is a contributing factor to our overconsumption.

Joe's Story

I have a huge sneaker collection. When asked to reflect on a moment in childhood that may have influenced me becoming a sneakerhead, I  immediately recalled the incident. New Jordans had been released, and like most children, I asked my parents to purchase a pair for me. At the time, sneakers that were almost one hundred dollars were unrealistic for many Black children, and my family was no exception. Instead of buying me the real Jordans, they purchased a pair of knockoffs. And not just any knockoffs, obvious knockoffs because in addition to the classic silhouette of Michael Jordan in mid-air about to dunk the basketball, there was the silhouette of another player blocking him. To make matters worse, I had to wear those ugly-ass knockoffs because my parents purchased them with their hard-earned money. Man, I got clowned at school! The jokes were never-ending, and I was so mad and resentful. The first real Nikes I got were in ninth grade. They were then mandated team basketball shoes, and I got yelled at by the coaches for wearing them daily off the court. Now that I am older, financially independent, and successful, I buy whatever pair of sneakers I want—and

you know what? I still think about those new Jordans. By
the way, after this exercise, I counted how many sneakers I
own. There are fifty-six pairs and out of those, twenty-nine
pairs are Jordans.

Acknowledging which aspects of your childhood have contributed to having more than you need is owning up to a powerful
truth. Later, these reflections will be a crucial part of the work of
forgiveness as you begin the "letting go" process. Sometimes, the
act of forgiveness will require us to do more than forgive ourselves
for making uninformed choices. Sometimes we must forgive the
people who taught us (or who we believe are responsible for) our
relationship to spending and acquiring more things than we need.

I do not blame my mother for my spending habits, nor the resulting excess. In addition to inheriting the generational trauma
of the Great Depression, her own childhood was so wrought with
heartache and grief from losing her mother as a teen that it remains
a period of her life that is too painful to discuss. What she experienced and how she managed these incidents resulted in coping
mechanisms that may have *influenced* my behavior, but ultimately,
the choices that I made and continue to make as an adult are mine.

"As the saying goes, once you know better, you have the
power and responsibility to do better."

—Christine

Now that I understand how my childhood influenced my
spending habits, I know what my triggers are and, more impor-

tant, how to respond to them. Although I have gotten much better at being disciplined, I still have moments of weakness. But this, too, is empowering because it allows me to continue developing strategies to curtail my excess spending. Often, these setbacks are due to the psychology of ownership and, in particular, the need to feel in control, something that became even more clear after making purchases during the COVID-19 pandemic. But thankfully, that is what returns are for!

A Note for Caregivers

As you reflect on and begin to better understand how your childhood influenced your adult behaviors and spending habits, consider how you may be emulating these behaviors in your own household. If you are able to identify any harmful practices, it may be time to have an honest conversation with your children on an age-appropriate level. This is one way to course correct and ensure that your children will make better and more informed decisions as adults.

We Want to Keep Up

Whether we want to admit it or not, most people care about what others think about them. Part of our socialization includes understanding the benefits of being held in high regard and seen as someone with an admirable reputation and image. Unfortunately, due to our current culture of consumerism, one's social status and even their worth as an individual is often assessed by looking at the tangible items they own. Inevitably, this results in people purchasing items because they want to impress others or because they believe that owning or wearing certain items will cause people to admire or respect them. People who engage in this type of spending are known as conspicuous consumers.

"Many people have more than they need to due to conspicuous consumption, which is the act of purchasing luxury items and wearing or displaying them in an attempt to enhance or give the appearance of prestige."

—Christine

The term "conspicuous consumption" was coined by an American economist named Thorstein Veblen. In his book *The Theory of the Leisure Class*, Veblen gives an in-depth historical overview of how the need to display one's wealth as a way to show superiority and power goes as far back as kings and queens flaunting gold-plated wares and having lavish, opulent parties that were unattainable to commoners. From celebrities wearing high-end fashion to driving automobiles more expensive than many residential properties, conspicuous consumption is a large part of the culture of consumerism made even more voyeuristic and ostentatious thanks to the popularity of social media.

We are constantly bombarded with enticing ads (and sales!) of the newest and best of everything. Our inboxes and social media feeds are flooded with new temptations. Coupled with this temptation are the people, or the more modern term "influencers," who acquire and display these things to entice others to purchase them (or who are engaged in their own act of conspicuous consumption!).

According to Veblen, one of the main causes for conspicuous consumption is the desire for peer recognition and the desire to assert a higher social status.[4] Many of us grew up with another term for conspicuous consumption—"keeping up with the Joneses."

If you are not familiar with the Joneses, they are a fictional family and one that appears to have acquired everything that encompasses the American dream. An impressive McMansion. Luxury cars. Designer clothing. Expensive jewelry. The latest technology. And, depending on who is trying to keep up with them, at least two perfect children playing in the front yard on luscious green grass surrounded by a white picket fence.

The Joneses are a stand-in for our ideal. They represent the perfect, want-for-nothing, magazine-ready life so many aspire to. They own things that are out of reach for most, yet they continuously, conspicuously consume to remind others of just how affluent they are. The Joneses always have the newest, the latest, and the greatest. And folks want to keep up with the Joneses because, well, maybe, just maybe, if they had what the Joneses have they would be respected and have perfect lives, too!

The Joneses are a true representation of conspicuous consumption—equal parts envy and admiration. And even though most people do not have the wealth to "keep up" with this fictional family, that does not stop them from trying at any cost. Even if it means taking on debt.

The Joneses symbolize not only our obsession with consumerism, but our obsession with wanting to purchase the most luxurious, expensive items to show others. "Look, we've made it, too!" For many people, having the latest and greatest fills an emotional void of needing to be accepted and respected by family, friends, neighbors, and even strangers. But this is a false sense of reality, a belief that unless one has these certain things, one hasn't quite "made it" by social standing. This falsehood is one of the underlying reasons people constantly buy new things, and more often than not, the most expensive things, in the hopes of proving their affluence or prestige.

Everyone wants to look like the Joneses, but they have no idea what financial stress the Joneses might be experiencing to maintain their persona. But that, too, doesn't stop people from trying.

Did You Know?

The average American has $90,460 in debt.[5] This includes all types of consumer debt products, from credit cards to personal loans, mortgages, and student debt.[6] Here are the average debt balances by age group:

1. Gen Z (ages 18 to 23): $9,593
2. Millennials (ages 24 to 39): $78,396
3. Gen X (ages 40 to 55): $135,841
4. Baby boomers (ages 56 to 74): $96,984
5. Silent generation (ages 75 and above): $40,925[7]

Millennials have seen the largest increase in debt in the last five years: In 2015, the average millennial had about $49,722 in debt, and by 2019 they carried an average of $78,396 in total debt—an increase of 58 percent.[8]

"Black conspicuous consumption comes from a deep need to heal generational wounds of unworthiness and lack. This is the legacy of white supremacy. We are predisposed to want things and stuff because of the internalization of beliefs that we are not enough until we are liberated from that mindset."

—Erin Trent Johnson, MPA, CPC

In the spirit of transparency, I, too, have been guilty of going into debt trying to keep up. While this behavior started in college on a smaller scale, it escalated significantly once I moved to a major metropolitan city. At the time, I had all sorts of ways to justify my spending, including the common conspicuous consumption rationale that I needed to "look the part." Expensive handbags. High-end designer clothing and shoes. A luxury car. I naively believed these things gave me a sense of belonging in my profession and among my peers, which of course they didn't. The truth is they were just things, expensive things. And that is why it hurt all the more seeing them among the huge piles of the belongings I didn't need.

Due to social media and online shopping, purchasing unnecessary items to impress others is now easier than ever and often results in people having more than they need and—even more troubling—more than they can afford. Additionally, the constant pursuit of trying to impress others can lead to unhealthy opinions of self-worth and self-esteem. Conspicuous consumption has deeper implications than an overflowing wardrobe and flashy personal effects.

Outsourcing our sense of self-worth to our belongings can result in a vicious cycle of always feeling less than because we can never have enough. Allowing others to judge us based on what we have or don't have coincidentally results in us judging ourselves. You will *never* be satisfied chasing after the next new thing, because once you acquire it, there will always be something new. That's the real truth about trying to keep up with the Joneses: It is impossible to ever catch up or keep up because the stakes are ever-changing.

Listen, there is nothing wrong with buying expensive things if that's what feels authentic to you (and you can afford them!). But as you work through your process of self-discovery, there may be times where you have to do some serious self-interrogation to uncover why you feel you simply must have certain items. There is no harm in having a favorite expensive skin care line that you can afford and use regularly because it feels like an expression of self-love and works well for your needs. But buying luxurious skin care products because of a social media ad with a popular influencer has you worried that your existing skin care regimen isn't "cool enough," is concerning. Much like our childhood experiences, conspicuous consumption can find its way into every area of our lives. In fact, it has always been there.

As Veblen noted, humans' desire to impress others has been around for centuries. From the kings and queens adorning themselves in gold and throwing lavish feasts in their castles, to Hollywood superstars giving us a glimpse into the "lives of the rich and famous," the flaunting of wealth is ingrained in our societal culture. The need to *show* people our lives has only been amplified by our online presence, resulting in many costly false narratives. But conspicuous consumption can even show up in the simplest of ways. Many people grew up in homes with fully furnished, immaculately decorated rooms . . . that no one except special guests were allowed to go in. In fact, there is one familiar sight that can be found in many American households—the sacred cabinet of porcelain dishes encased in glass that are on display for family, friends, and houseguests . . . and on display only.

Charisma's Story

Growing up, I loved looking at the china cabinet in our din- ing room. The dishes were so elegant, so pretty! But I could only look at them through the  glass because no one could touch them, let alone use them. And when I say no one, *no one*. Not even when my mother had dinners for her most esteemed guests did this china ever come out of the cabinet. I remem- ber wanting to eat off those plates so badly as a child. There was something about them being untouchable that let me know they were special. I kept waiting for me or one of my siblings to do something worthy enough, something spectacular enough to warrant my mother opening the glass and pulling out the fine china so we could celebrate by eating off those fancy dishes. Award- winning games. High school graduations followed by col- lege graduations. Marriages. The births of grandchildren. Here I am, now in my forties, and I realize there is no accomplishment great enough that will ever warrant us actually using those plates.

Due to the recent commodification of simplicity, conspicuous consumption has even found its way into the practice of living with less. Marketing and advertising follow the latest trends, and because minimalism continues to gain popularity, businesses have followed suit. All the more reason why your new lifestyle must be grounded in intentionality and authenticity. Otherwise, you may find yourself purchasing "minimalist things" in an effort to display your new lifestyle. (Side note: A "minimalist" product is a falsehood. These are rebranded items that are simply made for small spaces.)

So, how does one determine if they are being a conspicuous consumer instead of just being a person who likes nice things? The answer is rooted in the intention behind your actions. This requires an honest self-assessment to identify whether you purchase certain items because you like and can afford them or for the purpose of achieving a desired result—to display your wealth and power, or in the hopes of having others believe that you are wealthy and powerful.

Ask Yourself

Do I believe that owning certain items causes people to see or respect me differently? Do I base my decisions on what others may think once they know that I have acquired certain items?

Asking yourself these questions is the first step in determining whether your purchase is necessary or, instead, intended for some other reason that is more aligned with conspicuous con-

FOR THE CULTURE

▼▲▼▲▼

Conspicuous consumption is an especially important consideration for Black Americans and other marginalized communities. From designer clothing to expensive sneakers and luxury cars, displaying wealth or perceived wealth is very much a part of our culture. A recent Morning Consult survey found that 50 percent of Black consumers said they trust celebrities and athletes to give them good advice on brands, while 44 percent said the same of influencers.[9] Let's face it: Many people in the Black community allow others to dictate what we buy. We feel a sense of belonging and self-worth because we have the same things as people we admire.

First-generation college graduates and six-figure income earners can easily find themselves caught up in the dangerous web of conspicuous consumption. In addition to having the means to acquire luxury items that align with societal success, they also tend to feel a sense of responsibility and obligation to do so.

But how much more liberating to shift our perspective? How much more empowering and beneficial to instead view first-gen success as an opportunity to build generational wealth? As someone once tethered to the burden of trying to look the part, I now believe I have a responsibility to be intentional and forward-thinking with my resources. I also believe this is a small part of a larger collective responsibility to invest in our communities and build a lasting legacy for future generations, rather than spend on momentary expense trends that quickly lose their value and perceived prestige.

For example, did you know:

- 96.1 percent of the 1.2 million households in the top 1 percent by income are White.[10]
- America's 100 richest people control more wealth than the entire Black population.[11]
- The five largest White landowners own more land than all Black people combined.[12]
- The average Black family would need 228 years to build the wealth of a White family today.[13][14]

We have a choice of how, on what, and where we choose to spend our dollars. And sometimes that choice is as simple as choosing to give in to the temptation of conspicuous consumption or devoting our resources to more meaningful, long-term investments.

sumption. And believe me—I understand how difficult the exercise is. These questions can lead to uncomfortable conversations that no one wants to have, with ourselves or anyone else for that matter. But the truth is that we must.

Trust me, now that I know what I know, there are *so* many things that I would have done differently when it comes to spending so many years being a conspicuous consumer. There are times I even feel guilty for learning how to course correct so late in the game. But that is why I so passionately and sincerely share my truth. I want others to know what I wish I had known. I want you to understand the power and impact of your choices.

If conspicuous consumption is an area where you struggle, know that you have the ability to make different choices and commit to doing so today. Liberating yourself from wanting to keep up with the Joneses and seek validation by acquiring things will not only change your spending habits, but also how you determine your self-worth. This is one of the benefits of approaching minimalism through self-discovery: learning to find value not in what you have but, instead, in who you are.

The Pressures of Cultural Expectations

Depending on your ethnicity, nationality, familial status, and other social identities, there is a good chance that you have felt the pressures of cultural expectations. These widely accepted attitudes and beliefs are representations of the values, social norms, gender roles, birth order, or other factors of the communities and identities we are born into. Cultural expectations are so ingrained that sometimes, we even come to believe them ourselves. Other times, the pressures are so great that people feel they have no other alterna-tive, that the circumstances are out of their control. They *have to* buy an expensive property in the right zip code. They *have to* drive an expensive car. They *have to* acquire and do certain things because that is what is expected of them. Because these well-defined expec-tations, whether spoken or understood, carry just that much weight.

"What do you mean you don't like shopping? You're a woman! All women like to shop!"

"You're the first-born son, you know what's expected of you."

"You're a doctor and you live in an apartment? I thought all doctors were rich."

Even if we can acknowledge the stereotypes and falsehood embedded in cultural expectations, we often still conform to these beliefs. And based on how often they show up in our lives, we often feel compelled to comply accordingly. I know I sure did.

As the daughter born to a West Indian mother and a Jamaican father, I was very much aware of what was expected of me. It was little surprise to anyone that I became a first-generation college graduate and went on to pursue advanced degrees. That was what I was supposed to do—be great. And when I became the first six-figure income earner in my immediate family, that, too, came with expectations of what I was supposed to own, how I was supposed to look, and who I was supposed to help. I was the rich one (note, I was *not* rich). And therefore, I was expected to do what rich people do—spend (another note, that is *not* what rich people do!).

The more I begrudgingly (and sometimes, excitedly) com-plied with the expectation of being "the rich one," the more I spent. I was a lawyer. Weren't lawyers supposed to drive luxury cars, wear high-end clothing, and carry designer handbags? I was

FOR THE CULTURE

▼▲▼▲▼

One of the hardest things for me to accept was that cultural expectations, whether real or perceived, often play a role in our conspicuous consumption. This can be especially difficult to explain to people who are raised in households that favor and value individualism. It is not uncommon to hear, "You bought that because that's what *your mother* thinks you should buy? I would never!" But the reality is, these pressures are just as daunting, especially because of their intersectionality, and can lead to making us purchases for peer recognition or to denote our social standing not because *we* want to but rather, because that's what is expected of us.

Here are some points to consider while doing the inner work of determining whether you are engaging in conspicuous consumption based on cultural expectations:

1. Do you purchase things because your family or friends expect that someone with your level of education or credentials should have such things? For example, do you drive a luxury vehicle with

a hefty car note when you would prefer to ride a bike? Would choosing to do the latter bring shame and embarrassment to your family or cause you to be ridiculed by friends?

2. Have you acquired debt for things that you do not need or want because your family or friends expect that someone with your level of education or credentials should have such things? For example, do you own a large home in an upscale neighborhood when you would prefer to reside in an affordable one-bedroom apartment until you pay off your student loans?

3. Do you compromise aspects of who you are and what brings you joy because your family or friends expect that someone with your level of education or credentials should find joy in other things? For example, do you wear designer clothing and accessories, especially around family and friends? (Even though, no matter how hard you try, you struggle to tell the difference between a knockoff and the real thing!) Would choosing to have simple belongings that do not carry the prestige of designer items bring shame and embarrassment to your family or cause you to be ridiculed by friends?

a Black woman. Wasn't I supposed to go to the hairdresser every weekend and the nail salon every other week? I was raising my daughter in an affluent two-income household in the suburbs. Wasn't she supposed to have elaborate birthday parties and enjoy the lavish lifestyle I dreamed of as a child?

Otherwise, what would people think!

These expectations, coupled with my ability to spend extravagantly (at the sales rack) whenever I wanted to (okay, every payday, but you know what I'm saying), were definitely contributing factors to me acquiring things that I did not need as well as much more than I needed. And the pressure abounded until I pursued a new career in publishing: *Poor Christine. Of course she's wearing no-name ballet flats. You know she's a struggling writer now.*

Perhaps you are not even aware or don't realize some of the ways that the pressures of cultural expectations influence your spending. But as you reflect on when, what, and why you purchase certain things, their influences will surely become more apparent.

I recall having a conversation with a young Nigerian dentist after one of my workshops on the benefits of minimalism. She desired to live with less but unfortunately, she felt it was impossible because of cultural expectations both domestically and in her home country. This beautiful young woman was single but lived in a well-appointed four-bedroom town house with a mortgage that was eating away at her income. She confessed that she would be much happier in a one-bedroom apartment but was afraid of what her family would think of her decision. In fact, she was certain it would be frowned upon and deemed "unacceptable" for a woman with her credentials and societal standing. Without a doubt, she was not only feeling the pressures of cultural expecta-

FOR THE CULTURE

▼▲▼▲▼

"Live for Today Because Tomorrow Ain't Promised"

Much of the advice and many of the adages that Black people hold dear have been passed down generationally. They are woven into the fabric of our communities and have become a part of our cultural beliefs and inform our choices. But we must remember that some of our ancestors' guidance helped them withstand the systemic terror and oppression of their respective eras and thus is no longer applicable today. For example, the idea of saving seemed ridiculous when one could not be certain if they would meet death due to Jim Crow laws or some other act of state sanctioned violence. Why plan for tomorrow when you weren't certain you'd even make it home for dinner each day? Historically, there are so many reasons why our foremothers and forefathers lived for the moment—the moment was all that was certain. So, when they had enough money to buy what they wanted, it was best to make the purchase because "tomorrow ain't promised." Today, the learned behaviors of our ancestors and their advice to "live for the moment" continue to influence our relationships with money and impact opportunities to build generational wealth. Which is why we must continuously work to dismantle cultural beliefs that are no longer applicable and beneficial to our communities.

tions but also how giving in to these pressures resulted in her living an unhappy and inauthentic life. The only advice that I could give her was the hard truth: If she wanted to live her best life she had to do it on her terms.

Cultural expectations are difficult to manage because the pressure often comes from the people and communities who love us the most. In order to identify and begin dismantling cultural expectations that are impacting your spending you may need to have some difficult, honest conversations and set boundaries with family and friends. It is the only way that you can truly live an intentional, authentic life.

Mindless Consumption

Shopping out of boredom or for leisure is nothing new. It was surely a pastime for my mother and me during those wonderful weekend excursions I enjoyed as a child. Only today, there is one difference that has caused mindless consumerism to change from a simple pastime to a full-fledged economy, resulting in so many people having more than they need: the internet.

The ease of advertising to consumers whenever they open their phones to check their favorite social media apps or log on to their computers to browse the Web has resulted in a new way to shop to just pass the time: mindless consumerism.

We can get whatever we want (and whatever we don't need), whenever we want it. Our credit card or debit card information, as well as our shipping address, can be saved and auto-populated for added convenience. With the click of a button, whatever we decide to purchase in a moment of boredom is ours.

A simple reflection upon on my childhood always reminds me of just how quickly things have changed. Life was simple. Shopping was less complicated. And technology wasn't even a consideration.

The first gaming system that I owned was an Atari. As a child, we had a rotary phone, and I loved the feeling of turning that little wheel to each number I needed and waiting for what would now seem like eternity for an operator to connect the call. And I still remember when the first family in our neighborhood got a microwave, and all us kids were certain that within a year, cars would be able to fly and we would eat meals in pill form just like the Jetsons.

I listened to cassette tapes, and also used them to record my favorite songs from my pink Casio boom box. I had the first Walkman, and the first Discman, which resulted in me having more CDs than I could count that came in the mail thanks to me joining the Columbia Records CD Club.

In undergrad, I thought I was pretty hot stuff with my Brother word processor that could—gasp—erase what I'd just typed. I printed most of my college papers at the university library. And when I returned to my dorm room, I called my mother on the residence hall's landline using a prepaid phone card.

When it comes to technology, I once owned a pager (or beeper, if you wanted to be cool in these streets. Ha!). I also owned the first Nextel cell phone as well as the first BlackBerry, and the first-generation iPod Nano (which I *still* have, and it *still* works!)

I remember purchasing my first personal desktop computer, a Gateway, which was shipped to me in the mail *for free*. And my first personal laptop was so heavy, I literally had shoulder pains from carrying it around campus.

I could not believe when I could listen to voice mails on my

phone instead of waiting until I got home to listen to the messages on my answering machine. I'm pretty sure that in some
random box in my mother's garage you'll find all the ethernet
and other cables I needed to get online and watch television. And
don't even get me started on apps and whatnot because I am still
low-key in awe and amazement of everything we can do with a
mobile phone. Or is it a cell phone?

Whatever!

I grew up during an era when there were no debit cards, only
credit cards. If someone wanted to transfer, loan, or give money
to someone else, the transaction had to take place at their local
banking center. There were no financial apps to streamline the
process to make an exchange in seconds. If you wanted to do a
little shopping, you went to the store, and if the item you wanted
needed to be ordered, you knew it would be a while before it was
in your hands. Yes, people surely engaged in mindless consumption but certainly not at the feverish pace with which we do today.

I know, I know. You are probably wondering how I look so
good to be two hundred years old. Despite the technological advancements that have happened in my lifetime, I am not *that* old.

I was born in 1976.

This is just how quickly technology has advanced in less than
fifty years, and with it the ability for consumers to do what consumers do best: buy all the things.

Even though technological advancements have made life
much easier, they have also heavily impacted our spending habits.
Obviously, purchasing things that we want, need, and love is both
a practicality and necessity. But it is important to distinguish between these purchases, and equally important to determine when

and how these purchases are made to make sure you are not engaging in mindless consumerism.

Acknowledging your participation in mindless consumption will be an essential part of your journey to living with less. There will always be ads (and sales!) for goods and services that are designed to entice to you to spend, especially in those moments where you are just looking to pass the time. Through the intentional practice of owning only what you need, use, and love, you will learn to be content with what you have. You will also discover tactics that work best to curb your mindless consumption, such as committing to wait twenty-four to forty-eight hours before making purchases.

Ask Yourself

1. Is your credit or debit card information stored on your phone or computer solely for the ease and convenience of e-commerce?

2. Have you ever purchased something you hadn't planned on as a result of an online ad?

3. Do you frequently receive deliveries, and you can't remember when or why you purchased them?

Now that you have a more comprehensive understanding of the principles of minimalism as well as the reasons why you have more than you need, you are better prepared to take on the work ahead. Remember, eliminating your excess will not cure bad spending habits or behaviors. It is only one milestone on the journey to living with less. In order to maintain your practice, you will

FOR THE CULTURE

▼▲▼▲▼

It is not uncommon for people in marginalized communities to have unhealthy relationships with credit or even lack the knowledge of how it works, and lenders are fully aware of this demographic's vulnerability. Due to limited personal finance education, marginalized communities have long since been victimized by predatory lending. Today, there are many more barriers and protections in place to curb people obtaining more credit than they can manage as well as an abundance of free financial literacy courses. But keep in mind, lenders do not take into consideration non-tangible factors like your childhood experiences and the pressures of cultural expectations—banks look at your income and credit score as indicators of how much credit you are qualified to receive. Additionally, you may legally meet the requirements for the credit limit that you receive, but if not managed accordingly (which is what predatory lenders are counting on), you can easily find yourself in debt. And this can happen very quickly when you are actively engaged in mindless consumerism.

have to reflect on and remain mindful of your triggers and influences as you commit to being a more conscious consumer.

More and Less: A Brief Historical Timeline

It might be difficult to imagine that our foremothers and forefathers lived with less. A few centuries ago, there was no need to define minimalism as a lifestyle choice because not only was simplicity a way of life, less was *the* way of life.

People made their own goods and/or relied on systems and local bartering. Advertising was limited to word of mouth or paper billets. And there was little consideration given to one's social status because communities were so contained.

But with the discovery of natural resources, economies shifted from being agrarian to textile manufacturing. Innovations in transportation and technology soon followed. Advertising transitioned from paper billets to direct marketing through radio, television, and, later, the internet. E commerce opened up accessibility locally and globally and intensified the growing culture of consumerism by placing buying power in the hands of customers.

Despite modern-day efforts that encourage a return to simplicity, humanity continues to consume at a feverish pace, much to the detriment of our wallets and the environment. From fast fashion filling landfills to plastics polluting oceans, human overconsumption causes more harm than an overflowing, cluttered wardrobe.

So, how did we get here? The following brief historical overview of the four industrial revolutions provides insight on how society transitioned from one accustomed to and content with less to one always wanting more.

Pre-Industrial Revolution

Much of the world's economy is agricultural. Few
goods and clothing are purchased, and instead
are homemade and bartered locally. Transportation is limited to traveling by foot or horse/mule
and wagon. People rarely leave their communities
(and most certainly not solely to go shopping!).
People are not yet thought of as consumers but
rather as farmers or artisans until agricultural
technologies lead to large-scale production of
advanced farming. As a result of losing their land
and livelihoods, people begin to leave their familial lands and villages in search of opportunities in
urban cities.

First Industrial Revolution
(1750–1850)

The discovery of coal leads to new inventions
like the steamboat, allowing travel and transport
of goods by waterway. Traditional dirt roads are
paved with gravel, making travel easier by foot
and wagon. The largest transportation advance-
ment, the railroad, soon becomes the primary
mode to ship goods across the United States.
New inventions like mechanical sewing machines
cause a boom in factory-based textile industries,

FOR THE CULTURE

▼▲▼▲▼

Prior to the industrial revolution, enslaved Africans were forced to plant and harvest crops by hand. These laborious tasks only intensified with the invention of farming technologies and resulted in an increased demand for African slave labor and the destruction of indigenous lands. According to the Trans-Atlantic Slave Trade Database, between 1525 and 1866, an estimated 12.5 million Africans were shipped to the New World, with approximately 10.7 million surviving the dreaded Middle Passage and disembarking in North America, the Caribbean, and South America.[15]

in turn causing mass production of goods that were once homemade. Factory workers begin using their wages to purchase some of the very goods they were paid to manufacture, and the culture of consumerism begins to grow.

Second Industrial Revolution (1850–1970)

The discovery of oil, gas, and electricity increases manufacturing production and efficiency. Airplanes and automobiles also emerge during this era, allowing manufacturers to ship larger quantities of goods more quickly to an ever-growing market of eager consumers. The Great Depression results in generational traumas such as food scarcity and housing instability, causing survivors and their descendants to become extreme hoarders and savers throughout their lifetimes out of fear that they might lose everything once again. Post-Great Depression new forms of personal communication such as radios and televisions allow advertising through repetitious, targeted marketing efforts. And companies begin hiring movie stars and sports figures (hello, influencers!) to persuade Americans to purchase products.

FOR THE CULTURE

▼▲▼▲▼

During the second industrial revolution, racialized violence against Blacks accelerated after the abolition of slavery. Some of these incidents destroyed significant sources of generational wealth, such as the 1921 Tulsa Race Riots in Oklahoma, which resulted in the destruction of one of the wealthiest Black communities in America. The passing of racist legislation such as the GI Bill, which granted White World War II veterans access to low-cost mortgages, business loans, tuition assistance, and unemployment compensation, but excluded Black veterans, further contributed to already dire wealth disparities.

Third Industrial Revolution (1969–2000)

Advances in manufacturing technologies continue to improve with the discovery of nuclear and renewable energies. The invention of the internet allows consumers to have direct access to businesses through e-commerce and enhances globalization. The economic downturn during the Great Recession causes a momentary pause in consumerism. People begin to seek more economical and sustainable living solutions, and movements such as tiny houses and minimalism begin to emerge.

Fourth Industrial Revolution (2000–Present)

As our current industrial revolution continues to evolve, the discovery of solar, wind, and geothermal energy as well as digital technological advancements such as wireless networking technology continue to give consumers more purchasing power through Web-based retailers. Additional advancements such as robotics and artificial intelligence continue to merge our virtual and physical worlds and streamline e-commerce. We will have to wait to see just how deeply these advancements influence our culture of consumption.

why it's so hard to let go

Knowing the historical, societal, and cultural factors that contribute to people having more than they need is only part of the equation when it comes to living with less. There is another common denominator that can make adopting a minimalist lifestyle challenging: Sometimes, it's just really hard to let go of the things that we have.

Even those things we don't need.

Even those things we don't use.

Even those things we don't love.

Despite our best efforts, we just can't seem to part with them.

Throughout my journey, there were many items that I struggled to part with. Clothing and shoes that I couldn't remember the last time I'd worn. Kitchen gadgets and coffee mugs that I'd never used. Home goods and knickknacks that served no purpose (not even for decoration, because they were stored in drawers!). And don't even get me started on personal documents, journals, and notebooks.

I couldn't understand why I couldn't let certain things go even though they served no purpose in my life other than filling up usable spaces and storage with clutter. My search for answers to these questions led me to discovering an important issue that is rarely addressed in the minimalism movement: the psychology of ownership.

Most of us are familiar with the legality of ownership, which is legally having the right to claim something as ours. But the psychology of ownership is a bit more complex. It is the *feeling* that something is ours, and this feeling can be the result of believing something belongs to us or that it is a part of or an extension of us. Regardless of the rationale behind the feeling, the end result is the same: It causes us to develop strong emotional attachments to our belongings, even those things we don't need, use, and love, which is why we find it so difficult to let them go.

To see the psychology of ownership expressed in its simplest and purest form, we can watch children play. Young people are quite vocal about their feelings of ownership when it comes to certain things such as toys and books. When my daughter was a toddler, it was not uncommon to hear her cry out during a play-date, "Hey, don't touch that toy. It's mine!" And she truly believed this sentiment. Even though the toy was *technically* mine . . . because, I mean, I purchased it!

At school, children claim ownership of classroom objects, even though the true owners of the items in question are their teachers. We have seen children assert ownership in public spaces such as parks where the idea of "sharing" an enjoyable playground fixture seems impossible to bear. And if you have ever taken children to the store with you and allowed them to hold a toy (or even something nonsensical like a roll of toilet paper) as a distraction, you know all too well the crying that can occur when you inevitably arrive at the register and tell them to put it back.

"No! It's mine!"

While adults often become frustrated with children's sense of possessiveness, we are just as guilty of developing feelings for things and forming attachments to them. Yes, just as quickly as a child walking around the store for a few minutes with a roll of toilet tissue (because "touch" plays a powerful role in the psychology of ownership!). The difference is that instead of simply declaring something as ours, as adults we can fully exert our feelings of ownership by purchasing the item, which only deepens our attachment to it. So, when the time comes to consider parting ways with our beloved belongings, we are akin to children standing with our arms crossed and lips poked out in defiance: We don't want to let go of our things.

Brands are fully aware of the psychology of ownership. In fact, it is an essential component of sales and marketing. Companies know how and why people form attachments to things, and how feelings of ownership make it difficult for us to think reasonably and rationally. Which is why understanding how and why you form attachments will be instrumental during the letting-go process *and* in maintaining your minimalist lifestyle.

FOR THE CULTURE
▼▲▼▲▼

Ownership is an especially complicated matter for people of the African diaspora. From our ancestors being stolen and once owned as property to our need to have things so that we feel in control of *something* in our lives, Black people have a different, deeper relationship with our belongings. Additionally, our communities are still grappling with generational implications and inequities resulting from slavery, Jim Crow, redlining, and other state-sanctioned limitations on ownership. Without a doubt, our familial and collective histories continue to influence why we are so attached to our things. Black people and other marginalized groups must understand the powerful connection between the psychology of ownership and the false sense of security it often provides. Our desire to seek comfort in things is heightened when we live in a society where we constantly feel unsafe, at risk. Take special note of areas in your life where your attachments to and unwillingness to let go of certain things may be rooted less in the culture of consumerism and more in the culture of White supremacy. Although making such acknowledgments can be difficult and even painful, this work is necessary, not only for your minimalist practice but also for your survival and that of our communities. If our resources are used to purchase things for comfort instead of building generational wealth, we run the risk of not only remaining victims of systemic oppression, but even worse, contributing to it.

How and Why We Form Attachments

First, please know that having feelings of possession and a desire to exert control over things is normal. From childhood to our senior years, some of the things we allow into our lives become so important and meaningful, it is impossible for us not to become bound to the joy we experience simply by having them around. Whether it's our favorite blankie or a new cashmere throw, our deep attraction to comfort usually results in an even deeper attachment to our belongings which makes it very difficult for us to let them go.

Did You Know?

Businesses and brands regularly target customers with opportunities to touch as well as have control over their products to induce feelings of ownership. When we touch or are allowed to control a product by, say, test-driving a car, it can lead to feelings of partial ownership because we are responsible for the product, become determined to own it, or fear losing the opportunity to own it.

The real power (and danger) of attachment is how quickly it can develop. Sometimes, the mere act of *touching* an item can trigger feelings of ownership. This is the earliest stage of forming an attachment, a feeling of developing partial ownership.

It's almost yours!

The longer you hold the item or have it in your shopping cart, the more you begin to develop a desire to have full ownership, which also triggers fear of loss.

I have to buy this right now! If I put it back, someone else might purchase it!

More than likely, this new thing is something you don't need, will never use, and may not even love (you just picked it up because it was pretty or to give a closer look!). But you touched it. And with just that one touch you triggered a cascade of feelings of ownership—partial at first, then a yearning for full ownership. You feared losing the opportunity to own the thing, to make it yours, and so you purchased it.

Attachment: The Reason We Have All the Things

Now that you have a better understanding of how and why we form attachments, you can fully appreciate why it is a well-established marketing strategy. Businesses and brands consistently use tactics that trigger feelings of partial ownership. They know, "If we can just get customers to touch this thing, they are more likely to buy it."

It is the reason car salespeople encourage you to "take a test drive." Why retailers urge you to "try it on." Just touch the sleekness of this, feel the softness of that. As a consumer, you have to know the endgame: Brands and businesses want you to form an attachment to their products, so you feel the need to buy and make them yours.

And before we know it, our houses and wardrobes are filled with all the things.

Think of attachments as invisible bonds between us and our belongings. Likewise, our feelings are also bonded to these attachments—certain things in our possession evoke happiness, nostalgia, and comfort. That is why the mere thought of losing or being forced to part with them can trigger feelings of anxiousness and fear. So, we continue to hold on to things we do not need, use, and sometimes, no longer even love.

In extreme cases, the fear of letting go of things that someone has formed attachments to manifests as hoarding. Many of us cringe at the homes of hoarders on television, staring in disbelief at people's excessive clutter as they struggle to let go of items that seem useless. But when it comes to attachments, we exhibit that same behavior on a smaller scale. We hold on to items because of our fears, afraid to lose the positive or sentimental feelings our belongings cause us to have, or because we think we might need or use them in the future.

When one of my friends was starting her journey to minimalism, she faced many struggles when it came to letting go of some of her clothing, especially attire that was high-end fashion. Even though she never wore these items, she'd convinced herself that one day, just maybe she might need to wear them. As she worked through each closet in her home, she'd frequently call to tell me about something fancy she'd found, and we'd laugh about the reasons why she still owned it—price tag still attached and often having never been worn a single time, convinced that there was some forthcoming occasion where she'd need to look her best.

One day, she called to tell me about a beautiful, expensive ball gown that she'd purchased for a fraction of the cost. (Isn't it convenient how sales stickers are strategically placed so we can see just how much of a deal we are getting . . . on something we don't need?) She'd convinced herself that this lavish gown, with layers of glorious silk, lace trimmings, and detailed embroidery, needed to be saved for a special occasion. That is why, despite her having never received an invitation to a high-profile event that seemed "worthy enough" to wear the ball gown, it still hung in her wardrobe.

"I'd been saving it for something big," she said laughing. "You know, a party where I might get a chance to meet Oprah or Michelle Obama!"

Let's be honest. Most of the things we are saving for future use, like a party where Oprah or Michelle Obama is in attendance, aren't happening. And if by happenstance we do one day receive the invitation of our dreams, we can rent the attire we need to look and feel our best.

I remember sorting through my own wardrobe and coming across similar shenanigans. Some of the clothing that I owned and these reasons why I still owned them, despite having never or rarely worn them, were comical. I have never laugh-cried so hard in my life! But sometimes, our attachments to things aren't as funny or as easy as, say, coming across the collection of yoga clothes you purchased in the hopes they would help you get on the mat more often. (Hint: They won't. Guilty as charged here!) Sometimes our attachment to things is tied to another aspect of psychological ownership, the reason *why* we form attachments in the first place: our motivations to own certain things because we believe they will satisfy certain wishes, desire, or goals.

Understanding Our Motivations

As humans, we are wired biologically, socially, and psychologically and our behaviors motivate us to fulfill these needs. Our biological motivations include buying water and food to satisfy our hunger and thirst. Socially, we are motivated to engage with others and form meaningful relationships with our family and friends because it is essential to our survival—rarely do people survive on their own. But it is our psychological motivations that most affect the forming of attachments to our belongings. We are motivated to have things that help us feel safe and secure, reflect our self-identity, and stimulate our senses.

There are four key motivators that cause us to have attachments to our belongings. Two of these motivators, (1) effectance, which stems from our need to understand and predict aspects of our lives to reduce uncertainty, and (2) stimulation, which stems from our need to feel aroused and stimulated, tend to play minor roles when it comes to our overconsumption. The remaining two motivators, (3) self-identity and (4) home, often take center stage when it comes to having more than we need because they cause us to acquire things that represent who we are and that brings us a sense of comfort and security, respectively. That is why it is important to understand how they work in concert with forming attachments to our belongings. And why we find it so hard to let certain things go.

Self-Identity:
Things That Represent Who We Are

One motivation that we are all familiar with is self-identity, our need to define and express ourselves to others. When it comes to our belongings, we consume in ways that are consistent with our self-identities. Whether it is a particular brand that represents our commitment to only buy ethically or sustainably, or holding on to our high school cheerleading uniform, we develop attachments to our belongings because we feel they are extensions of who we are, what we value, and what matters most to us.

As the Afrominimalist, I am motivated to purchase and own items that show my love for the history and beauty of the African diaspora. From Ankara-print clothing to mud-cloth-covered throw pillows, these items reflect my self-identity. As a result, they are much harder to let go of than items that have a more Eurocentric aesthetic.

When the time comes for you to "let go," you may find yourself being unable or unwilling to part with certain items you believe represent some aspect of your identity, whether presently or in the past. That is, after all, why you were motivated to buy or keep them. This doesn't mean that you can't keep some of them. But if you want to live with less, you can't keep *all* of them. You will have to work through your fears and decide which things you truly need, use, and love. And, most important, remember that things are not the only or even the best representation of our self-identity. Our work and contributions to society and our communities are some of the best ways to show who we are, what we value, and what matters most to us.

Home:
Things That Represent Comfort and Security

When it comes to understanding home as a motivation to have and keep things, this includes but also extends beyond our physical residences. When home is our motivator, our dwellings and belongings stem from our need to feel anchored. And our attachments are rooted in our desires to feel comfortable, safe, and secure.

Afrominimalism as Home

There are many things throughout my home and wardrobe that make me feel grounded and secure in who I am and what I love. Although it is easier to understand home and its décor as providing a sense of security, familiarity, and comfort, home as motivation also extends to items such as clothing, shoes, and accessories. My infamous orange jumpsuit, which I've worn to important events, such as my TEDx talk, or lounging or even to a casual brunch, is a representation of home as a motivation. It is recognizable, puts me at ease, and makes me feel confident and secure in my appearance.

If you are a member of the AfroMini community or have watched my TEDx talk, I am sure you are smiling. There is no other article of clothing that I have worn more often (and more proudly) than my favorite orange jumpsuit. Even if we consider self-identity as motivation, it is easy to see how my attachment to this article of clothing is because it is an extension of my Afrominimalist persona.

When the time comes for you to "let go," you will discover that you have formed attachments to some of your belongings because home is the motivation behind why you purchased and have them. But again, you will have work through your fears in releasing them, which will be especially difficult when it comes to those items that offer security and comfort. It is not uncommon to feel anxious at the thought of doing so. In fact, it is so common that it is another aspect of psychology—the understanding that some of our possessions cause us to feel a certain physical and psychological comfort, a way to make us feel safe in an unstable and uncertain world.

The problem with allowing our belongings to serve as sources of comfort is that we run the risk of setting unrealistic expectations for our things to provide certainty. This may be true momentarily but is an impossible standard to maintain. Because, well, life happens. Therefore, even our most cherished things can only provide a false sense of security. The reality is they can be taken away from us—whether through theft, an accidental fire, or natural disaster—at any time.

When it comes to our belongings—the motivations behind why we have them as well as our attachments to them—we have to learn to surrender. We have to learn to let go if we want to live with less.

Psychological Ownership and Consumerism

You might be surprised to know that the primary sources for my research on the psychology of ownership were not written by psychologists. Rather, I discovered this information by reviewing marketing and sales materials, because businesses and brands have already done the bulk of the research when it comes to understanding the psychology of ownership, motivations, and how people form attachments. Every year, they spend countless resources studying trends and finding ways to create and market their products for one main reason: so that consumers are motivated to purchase their products and form attachments to their brands (*hello, self-identity motivation!*).

As you prepare to begin the process of letting go, it's important to remember the reasons why you have more than you need and why it's so hard to let go. This will help ensure that you don't fill your newly cleared spaces with more things. Throughout your journey to living with less, you must always keep in mind the power of psychological ownership as it relates to you as a consumer.

Remember

1. You are wired for and constantly motivated to fulfill your biological, social, and psychological needs.
2. The mere act of touching an item triggers feelings of partial ownership, which can quickly lead to a desire to have full ownership, which also triggers fear of loss.
3. Once an item is in your possession, it is likely you will form an attachment to it. Attachments are like

invisible bonds between you and your belongings, and your feelings are also bonded to these attachments—you are happier simply by knowing certain things are in your possession.

4. The mere thought of losing or being forced to part with something you have formed an attachment to can trigger feelings of anxiousness and fear. This causes you to continue to hold on to things you do not need, use, and sometimes, even no longer love.

5. If you want to live with less, you will have to learn to surrender your fears and let go of things that no longer serve you.

Without a doubt, we all have things in our possession that we have formed attachments to, which is not always harmful, especially if you need and use these items. And of course, forming attachments to things is not the only reason for our overconsumption. But understanding the psychology of ownership is an integral part of the equation for recognizing why you have more than you need as well as why it's so hard to let go.

These truths are but one aspect of your self-discovery on your journey to living with less, which I want you to know is unlike any you have undertaken, because although there is a starting point—understanding the principles of minimalism—there is no destination. You are just beginning your adventure of committing to an authentic, intentional life.

a journey without
a destination

When it comes to living with less, the familiar adage "commit to the journey, not the destination" is indeed accurate. It is, first and foremost, a commitment to the principles: minimizing your excess to ensure your life is filled with only what matters. You are making a choice to be a more mindful consumer, to make decisions that are purposeful and that serve the person you are and the life you live. This is why minimalism is a journey with no destination. By committing to this lifestyle, your journey—much like you—will always be in progress. There are few steadfast rules, except your commitment and understanding that (1) you must always keep going and (2) you will always be growing.

Even though minimalism encourages simplicity, there will be

moments throughout the process that will not be easy, because, again, this is a process of self-discovery, and when we delve deeper into understanding who we are, what motivates our decisions and behaviors, we may discover aspects of ourselves that aren't easy to accept. But this work is also necessary for our evolution, our ability to acknowledge and commit to those areas of our lives where we want to change. Surely, minimalism is about letting go of things you don't need to make space for what matters. But these benefits go beyond your home décor and wardrobe.

Minimalism is the gateway to living an authentic, intentional, and purpose-driven life.

As my dear friend and fellow minimalist Courtney Carver of Mindful Simplicity and Project 333 often says, "The great thing about minimalism is that when you really dig in, you realize that when you live with less, your life becomes more than you ever imagined."

This is your journey, a way to learn to live with less on your terms. And although I am serving as your guide, this experience should not be rushed. You will experience many emotions along the way, and at times, you may even find yourself wanting to give up, because growth, while beautiful and necessary for us to become the best versions of ourselves, is difficult. Please know that it is okay to pause from the process or the practice whenever it becomes too overwhelming. But just pause, don't stop. Remember your commitment to the journey and why you chose this new path to personal liberation.

As you prepare to begin the process, I want to congratulate you for making a personal commitment to be a more mindful consumer. Be prepared to receive inquiries about why you have changed as curious minds may have questions about your new commitment to living with less (tell them!). But, most important, be prepared (and **excited**) as you pursue a life that is full of so much more.

More time.

More resources.

More authenticity.

More intention.

And best of all, a life comprising less of what no longer serves you and more of what makes you *you*.

part two

THE PROCESS

Congratulations on making it to the next phase of your journey to living with less, perhaps the one you have been most excited for. You've already accomplished the feat of learning about and identifying the reasons why you have more than you need, and you understand the psychology of why it's often so hard to let things go. Your reflections of self-discovery will come in handy as you prepare to confront how you got to this place in your life and to move forward. Now it is time to get to work!

Let me assure you, the process of letting go *is* work. From discovering what you need, use, and love among your many belongings to paying it forward with those that no longer serve, you are about to embark on a truly emotional and laborious experience. But the rewards are worth it—you will be that much closer to fulfilling your goal to live with less.

Many surprises await. And what's most exciting is that these surprises are about and will benefit *you*! As you strip away the excess in your home and wardrobe, I promise you will learn more about yourself than you ever thought possible. I know I did. Letting go led me not only to a new lifestyle but to discovering the depths of my capacity for creativity and pursuing my life with authenticity and intention.

When I reflect on my minimalist journey, I know exactly where many of you will be as you begin the process: standing in front of piles of your belongings, experiencing a storm of emotions from anger and frustration to disappointment and disbelief. I know all too well how it feels to be overwhelmed, ready to be a minimalist, but not sure what to do next as you prepare to part with many things that you once thought you couldn't live without.

Where does one start? When does one stop? And what does one do with all the stuff that's no longer needed?

Pause. Take a deep breath.

Remember, this is a journey. And as your guide, I am going to take you step by step through the process. It is one of the most pivotal stages of your minimalist practice, expanding on the self-discoveries you uncovered as you learned more about the principles of minimalism. The process of letting go will inform your new lifestyle for years to come.

The results of my own experiences led me to develop a holistic, tactical, four-step approach to eliminating the excess to make space for what matters. Each step is grounded in the principles and is designed to help you address how to acknowledge and let go as well as address the emotions that you are likely to experience—because, let's face it, this process is just as much about transforming your mindset as it is about transforming your home—as you learn to make space in your life for the things that feel authentic, necessary, useful, and loving.

step one	Acknowledge You Have Too Much
step two	Forgive Yourself
step three	Let Go!
step four	Pay It Forward

As you work your way through each step, imagine me by your side cheering you on with words of encouragement and affirmation. This work may feel daunting, and without a doubt, there will be moments where you are challenged in ways you never anticipated. But if you commit to this process, I promise that on the other side you will find a life filled with the kind of simplicity, authenticity, intention, and self-love that you have always wanted. It is the life that you deserve!

Remember, this process is as personal as minimalism itself. So, whether you go it alone or work in tandem with loved ones, remember to be firm about your end result and what brings *you* joy.

The Importance of Language

The Process of "Letting Go"

Although I prefer to use the terminology "letting go," the process of releasing what no longer serves you has many different titles. Decluttering. Organizing. Tidying up. You can call the process whatever you like, but there is one term I would like you to strongly consider avoiding: "purging." And I say this out of respect for our belongings and respect for ourselves. "Purging" has so many connotations of shame, disgust, and violence; of exorcism, and of things that are undesirable and unwanted. Please show love to your past self. Minimalism is about growing bigger in soul and spirit. Avoiding words that can trigger unhealthy thoughts and emotions is empowering as you embark on a healthy, holistic approach to building a sustainable minimalist lifestyle.

Some items will be much easier to let go of than others. If you find yourself struggling to part with certain items, simply put them aside. You can always come back at a later time to work through the reasons for your attachment or feelings of loss aversion. There were many items, especially in my wardrobe, that I had difficulty letting go until a later date and there is no reason to add extra stress by trying to part with items that you are not quite ready to release.

Keep in mind, too, that this is *your* journey. And it is a lifelong one. You're not a "better" minimalist because you let go of every-thing all in one weekend; you're not going to be happier because you rushed and made yourself let go of your granny's quilt, a designer sweater, or a collection of figurines before you were ready. Do you really want to spend the rest of your life regretting a hurried deci-sion that may have been different if you'd just taken your time?

Depending on your needs and goals, you may be fully capable of letting go of what no longer serves you quickly. If you are in the midst of moving across the country or downsizing to a smaller home, you may not have the luxury of extra time. Depending on your needs and preferences, you can take one of two approaches to this process: (1) quick, fast, and in a hurry or (2) slow and steady. Keep in mind that one approach may work well in one area of your home but not necessarily in another. Only you know which approach is best for you.

Two Approaches to Letting Go

Quick, Fast, and in a Hurry

I came across this approach early in my journey while searching for ways to just get the process over with. Of course, I had no idea at the time that minimalism is a lifelong commitment. Regardless, as soon as I saw this approach, I knew it would never work for me. Still, this is a great way to let go of what no longer serves you if (1) you have few attachments to your things, (2) you have no time to worry about attachments, or (3) you just need the get the job done... quick, fast, and in a hurry.

With this approach, simply fill boxes or bags with the items you think you no longer need, use, or love. Then seal them and store them out of sight for a period of time that works best for you (one to three months max) and commit to only opening them if there's something you need. If you don't find yourself needing to go into the boxes or bags, donate them (unopened!) when the time period ends.

Slow and Steady

After believing that I had the capacity to take on the letting-go process quick, fast, and in a hurry (and failing miserably), I decided to take the slow and steady approach. Whether it's committing to letting go of one item per day or tackling one room or drawer every weekend, the objective here is taking your time. This approach affords you the opportunity to really think about and consider what items you need, use, and love. Of course, the challenge with this approach is the same thing that makes it beneficial—it will take time. It took almost a year for me to finally complete the initial process of letting go, but as a result, I have no regrets.

Lastly, remember that the option to commit to this process is a privilege. Although the physical and emotional labor involved may not be easy, remember that having the choice to live with less is a privilege. The World Bank recently noted that global extreme poverty is expected to rise for the first time in more than twenty years as the disruption of the COVID-19 pandemic compounds the forces of conflict and climate change, which were already slowing poverty reduction progress.[1] In 2017, 24.1 percent of the world lived on less than $3.20 a day and 43.6 percent on less than $5.50 a day.[2] Living with less should not be another form of conspicuous consumption or a form of glamorized poverty. It is a lifestyle that you have chosen to pursue for the many benefits that it can offer you. Be grateful you have the choice. Be mindful of that choice. And use your privilege wisely.

step one

ACKNOWLEDGE YOU HAVE TOO MUCH

By this point, I hope it's safe for me to assume that you believe you are somewhat aware of your overconsumption. After all, you are reading a guide about learning how to live with less. But what does it mean to fully *acknowledge* that you have too much?

Throughout your life, there may have been times that you've felt you had too many things. You may have even expressed as much to yourself or laughed about this truth with friends in casual conversation. But calling yourself out for your collection of Glassybabies or your shoe addiction and acknowledging your excess for the purpose of starting the process of letting go is quite different.

Seriously, how much stuff do you *really* have?

Where Do I Start?

I know, I know. You want me to tell you exactly what to do. Beginning the work of letting go can feel daunting when your entire living space is beckoning you. But in all honesty, it is up to you to decide where you want to begin the part of your journey based on the time you have, the approach you've chosen, and your capacity to see it through. Because the process is overwhelming for most, I recommend selecting a small segment of your home to begin with. As you work through one area, you definitely become more confident to move to the next. But this is also an exercise in prioritizing. What area of your life do you want to release things from *right now*? For me it was my wardrobe. But for you it could be your kitchenware or your overflowing novel collection. Trust me, you will find your groove and what works best for you as you continue to sort through your belongings. Whatever you decide, allow yourself to start with the best intentions, and remember to extend yourself some grace along the way.

There's a reason acknowledgment is the first step in the process rather than jumping straight into the task of letting go. In order to live with less you must own up to the truth of your overconsumption. You've done the work to understand why you have more than you need and you know that you may struggle to part with certain belongings due to attachments. Now it's time to acknowledge just how much you actually have.

For more personal items like home goods and knickknacks, you can simply take them from where they are on display or out of their hiding places so you can truly see just how much you own. But for those areas where you know you have the most things, I am going to challenge you to a bit more labor-intensive work: take a full, written inventory of what you own. Yes, all of it.

Please understand that the purpose of this exercise is not to torment you. It serves a very important objective. We all have "our thing," those one or two areas in our lives where we are most prone to overspending and having excess. In order to acknowledge this truth, you must confront it by seeing just how much you really have.

For some people, this may be an antique collection, overflowing bookshelf, or an abundance of kitchen gadgets that promised to make mealtimes easier (spiralizer and egg cooker, anyone?). For others, it might be their affinity for makeup and grooming products. But most people will find themselves in their closets, dresser drawers, and wherever else they store their clothing, shoes, and accessories. The wardrobe is one area where many people *know* they have more than they need and are usually ready to make some changes. Such was the case for me, and I am excited to share how the acknowledgment process worked.

Despite what you may have seen on television, please know that the likelihood of you completing this process in an hour or less is unrealistic. Confronting reality takes time. So, plan accordingly!

Acknowledgment in Practice

No matter where you choose to begin, start by removing every-thing from its hiding place so that you can truly see what you own. Sometimes, just seeing all of your belongings laid out before you can be enough to acknowledge you have too much. In my personal practice, though, I took this a step further by doing a complete inventory of the one area of my life where I knew I had too much stuff: my wardrobe.

Not only did it help me acknowledge my affinity for bargain shopping, but it also served as a reminder of where I never wanted to be again. Even though I knew I had a lot of jeans, the reality of my excess hit differently once I counted more than fifty pairs. There's acknowledging that you have "a lot of jeans" and there's the acknowledgment of understanding that you have fifty-three pairs of jeans but only wear the same two.

Removing every article of clothing from its storage space also served another unexpected purpose: I realized that dressers and baskets were just additional places for me to conceal my excess—not functional systems of organization. As a result of discovering the number of items I had hidden and tucked away out of sight, I no longer own a dresser or nightstands with drawers. As I ac-knowledged just how much I had, I realized these storage solu-tions served as nothing more than opportunities to have space to accumulate more things I didn't need, use, or love.

Here is the inventory for my main closet that was in our mas-ter bedroom. (Keep in mind that I still had several other closets in our former home to work through!)

Shoes
- Heels: 31 pairs
- Boots: 12 pairs
- Flats: 16 pairs
- Sneakers: 5 pairs

Shirts
- Long sleeve T-shirts: 37
- Short sleeve T-shirts: 56
- Blouses: 44
- Sweatshirts: 22

Pants
- Jeans: 53
- Sweatpants: 21
- Other: 34

Workwear
- Dresses: 64
- Suits: 39

Workout Clothes
- Yoga pants: 26
- Sports bras: 15
- Tops: 22

(Note: Buying cute workout clothes will not make you work out!)

Accessories
- Purses: 39
- Scarves: 21

Total: 557 items

Whew! And to think, not only does this list not take into consideration my belongings that were stored in other closets and containers, but it also does not include all of my undergarments, nightwear, and accessories!

As difficult as this process was, it helped me acknowledge just how much I truly owned. I believe this is an essential first step because (1) knowing exactly what you have (and what you have too much of) forces you to acknowledge your excess and overconsumption; and (2) knowing exactly what you have (and what you have too much of) will help you make better choices going forward. After you complete your inventory, it's a good time to revisit your self-reflections that you discovered while learning about the principles of minimalism. Are you able to identify aspects of your childhood that have contributed to why you have more than you need, especially in one particular area? Are you able to identify areas where you are most prone to mindless consumption or conspicuous consumption? How much of your excess is due to giving in to cultural expectations rather than being your authentic self? This, too, is an important part of the acknowledgment process, because the answers to these questions allow you to see where you are most vulnerable, and, more important, what areas you need to address as you move forward in the journey to living with less.

As I've shared, acknowledgment was very difficult for me. I wasn't just confronting my stuff—I was confronting myself. Acknowledging just how much I had forced me to ask and answer those tough questions and face the reality of my spending habits and behaviors. With everything on display and categorized, many items with the red clearance tags still attached, I was able to fully understand how my childhood experiences and giving in to cultural expectations to "look the part" had resulted in me being extremely unintentional with purchases and careless with my resources.

Those little red clearance labels held the clues to my over-consumption—indicators of my obsession with finding a deal. Through the acknowledgment process I discovered and had to accept that bargain shopping was my Achilles' heel. It was clear that I was in love with the thrill of the hunt but once I got the items home, the dopamine rush subsided and the items went to their respective places of storage. There were so many new but unneeded, unused, and unloved items in my wardrobe! I knew I loved bargain shopping, but I had no idea how much of a contributing factor it was to my excess until I saw and acknowledged it.

Likewise, you will also come to see there are many layers (no pun intended!) when it comes to reasons why you have more than you need. Much like me, you may discover that although there may be one main contributing factor to your overconsumption, there are other areas that also play a role in your excess. As I reflected on my self-discoveries while acknowledging how many of my belongings I did not use, need, and love, I experienced a range of overwhelming emotions. I was so sad, so disappointed, and so angry with myself and my choices. Through tears and rage, I realized it would be impossible to move forward with letting go unless I acknowledged not only my overconsumption but also my feelings regarding how I had arrived at this place of having so much more than I needed. Which is what led me to develop Step Two: Forgiveness.

Before You Begin the Acknowledgment Process, Ask Yourself:

1. Do I have the time to take on the labor that will be involved in acknowledging how much I own? If you do not have hours to devote to the area of your life that is in the most need of attention, you may have to consider starting with a less challenging area until you do have hours to devote to the task. Unsure if you have the time or fear starting with a large undertaking, consider starting with something as simple as your spice cabinet!

2. Do I have the capacity to take on additional emotional stress? If you recently overcame an emotional challenge or are currently dealing with other emotional distress, now may not be the best time to start this process. You want to be in a good headspace so that you can fully commit to the acknowledgment process, not cause yourself more discomfort by being overwhelmed.

3. Is there someone who can help me? Whether it is your partner, close family member, or a dear friend, consider soliciting the help of people you trust to provide emotional support. In extreme cases such as hoarding, consider seeking the support of a licensed therapist to help you through the acknowledgment process.

Consider Bringing in the Professionals

There is no shame in knowing that you simply don't have the time, capacity, or wherewithal to manage this process without some help. Be honest with yourself regarding your abilities to commit to what may ultimately be a significant undertaking. If you have the resources, consider hiring a professional to assist you through the process. But remember, this is not a way to avoid doing the work of acknowledgment. Certified decluttering and organizational specialists can *assist* with helping you acknowledge your overconsumption as well as provide strategies to ensure you don't repeat the same behaviors and offer solutions to maintain your new lifestyle. But accepting the truth about your excess is ultimately your responsibility.

How do you know you are done with the acknowledgment phase of the process? Just as it is with your minimalist journey, there is no finality. Understand that this may be your first assessment of many, but as with most things, the first time is usually the most challenging. Once you have done the work to see and acknowledge just how much you have, and the emotions come flooding, it is time to move on to Step Two. Remember, you will repeat this process as you move through each area of your life where you want to live with less.

Let's Recap:
The Acknowledgment Process

- Acknowledgment is the first step we must take in our journey to let go of what no longer serves us.
- Acknowledgment allows us to own up to the truth of our overconsumption by forcing us to see just how much we have that we do not need, use, and love.
- Acknowledgment is a lesson in self-discovery, an opportunity to identify and address those areas where we are most vulnerable. This awareness is vital as we commit to the journey to live with less.

step two

FORGIVE YOURSELF

Rarely is forgiveness an easy action to take. This is largely because it usually centers on some form of hurt or wrongdoing. Often, we think of forgiveness in terms of an extension of grace that we give to others, people we care for enough to allow them another opportunity or a chance at redemption. Because of our emotional nature, it can be hard to extend such a generous offering of compassion to others. And surprisingly, it can be even more difficult to extend it to ourselves.

The overwhelming emotions that you encounter as part of acknowledging that you have more than you need may not wait until you are done with taking inventory. They can emerge at any time, rushing over you in waves, threatening to bring you to your knees. In those moments, it may be difficult to think about forgiveness, let alone extend it to yourself. But you have to. It's the only way you can move forward in your journey to live with less in a healthy way.

So, before we move to the process of letting go of the abundance of things you've just acknowledged you own, let's first work through letting go of the feelings that you are sure to experience. It's time to forgive yourself.

Andrea's Story

What surprised me the most as I acknowledged how much I owned were all the feelings I experienced. When I started sorting through my closet, I  was so excited! I turned on my favorite music and made sure my favorite bottle of wine was nearby. But the piles of clothing grew higher on my bed, then overtook my bed so I had to start making additional piles on the floor. The inventory list got longer, and I started to feel so sad. I found myself mentally calculating all the money I had wasted. I was also seeing so many pieces from my past that were tied to emotional spending. Like the dress I had purchased when I broke up with my ex only to wear it to an event that I knew he would be at in the hopes of making him see just what an amazing woman he had lost. There was a pantsuit I had worn to my high school reunion... and had not worn since. Fast fashion from vacations. High-end fashion that no longer fit (and was unlikely to ever fit again) that I was

still holding on to just because of the name on the label.
Before I knew it, I was sobbing.

I know the feelings Andrea experienced all too well. And I imagine that by this point you do, too. The guilt, the embarrassment, the unhappiness, the fury, the yearning and wishing that I made different choices—so many varied feelings emerged that it's nearly impossible to adequately describe what I felt as I acknowledged that I had so much more than I needed. There were times that I was overcome with extreme sadness. Other times I was so angry that I was shaking. And the one emotion that arose more than any other was disappointment. In fact, there were moments that I was so frustrated and upset with myself that I had to take a break.

Forgiveness may seem like an odd step in the letting-go process but trust me, it is essential. If you want to live with less, you must forgive yourself for the choices you made in the past. And understand that sometimes, the grace that you give to yourself may also have to be extended to others.

Forgiveness in Practice

During my self-discovery and acknowledgment of how my childhood weekend shopping excursions with my mother influenced my spending, I was never angry with her. She remains one of my best friends and is certainly not the shopper that I perceived her to be as a child. She has a near-perfect credit score and is one of the most frugal people I know. We frequently laugh at how she'd rather drink the last few drops of the coffee I've brewed than see me toss it down the drain—she only drinks decaf, by the way, and I most certainly need all the caffeine I can get.

Still, I thought of her during the acknowledgment process as well as other people in the Black community who influenced my decisions and desires to acquire certain things. I wanted and wished for so much more financial literacy and awareness, for us individually and collectively. It hurt to think about the amount of money that I had spent on useless things instead of taking vacations with loved ones or investing in a Black-owned start-up. I began seeing every article of clothing, every pair of unworn shoes and rarely carried designer handbag, every piece of tarnishing jewelry as dollar signs—money wasted, missed opportunities. And these feelings hurt and seemed a heavier burden than all the others.

What could I have done with all that money instead of wasting it on things?

This thought immobilized me. I sat on the bed next to all the things and cried. I walked over to the piles of stuff on the floor and kicked them in anger. I had never been so saddened and enraged and disappointed in my behavior. Rather than continuing to move forward with the process, these feelings held me captive. And the longer I sat with them, the more I felt bound.

I had made many, many mistakes. But there was truly nothing more that I could do than accept the humbling, disappointing truth and commit to making different choices going forward. But in order to do so, I had to forgive myself. And that forgiveness had to extend to my mother, who enjoyed spending the weekends shopping with her daughter, not knowing how it might influence her spending behaviors as an adult. I had to forgive the friends I frequently shopped with and the friends who couldn't see or were unwilling to tell me that I had a problem. Lastly, I had to forgive members of my community for not having the knowledge and awareness to show and teach me something different, whether it was because they didn't know or didn't feel it was their responsibility.

It was only through these acts of forgiveness that I was able to truly move forward with my commitment to live with less, which now included a commitment to be as honest and transparent as possible in an effort to help others avoid making the same mistakes.

You already know forgiveness will be difficult. This is likely not the first time in your life where you've had to dig deep to find the courage and compassion to extend it to yourself or others. However, when it comes to forgiving yourself for having more than you need, expect it to be especially difficult at times, because no matter the reasons we uncover during the process of self-discovery, we are solely responsible for our excess. No one forced us to buy more than we needed. Ultimately, the decision was ours and ours alone. As such, forgiveness is our responsibility to bear. And our reminder to do our best to never find ourselves in a similar situation again.

Reflecting, Forgiving

If you find it difficult to begin the process of forgiveness, I invite you to use the following reflection to begin this important work. Although I am a firm believer in the power of speaking words aloud and into existence, forgiveness is a personal matter so feel

FOR THE CULTURE
▼▲▼▲▼

For people of the African diaspora and other marginalized communities, the complexities of our history and family dynamics can easily lead to us blaming others for behaviors and spending habits that have contributed to our excess. Therefore, it is important that your forgiveness extend to your caregivers and your community as well. Extend grace to anyone who helped raise you and understand that they may have been doing the best they could under the circumstances, whether it was due to lack of education, resources, or guidance. Practicing forgiveness is an opportunity for you to acknowledge these challenges and complexities . . . and to make a decision to do things different going forward. And not just for yourself, but for your descendants and community as well. Consider these words by indigenous writer Tommy Orange as part of this process:

"What we are is what our ancestors did. How they survived. We are the memories we don't remember, which live in us, which we feel, which make us sing and dance and pray the way we do, feelings from memories that flare and bloom unexpectedly in our lives like blood through a blanket from a wound made by a bullet fired by a man shooting us in the back for our hair, for our heads, for our bounty, or just to get rid of us."
—Tommy Orange, *There There*

As you work through the many extensions of forgiveness that you may have to give to family members and friends, remember many choices and beliefs are remnants of what our ancestors had to do to survive. So, forgive. And commit to making different choices to benefit our community, individually and collectively.

free to honor this process in whatever way works best for you, such as writing letters of forgiveness in a journal or holding the forgiveness in your heart. The lesson here is not *how* to forgive, but rather to commit to the actual act of releasing any feelings and emotions that may keep you bound to your past.

As I commit to my journey to live with less, I acknowledge that I have more than I need and forgive myself for the choices that have led to my excess. I also forgive others who have, knowingly or unknowingly, contributed to my behaviors and spending habits, and I release any and all negativity that I may be harboring as a result of their influence. I have a right to experience everything that I am feeling. So, I allow myself to acknowledge these feelings, but I refuse to let them hold me captive and bound to my past. As I continue to do the work to live with less, whenever I feel negative emotions, I will acknowledge them. And then, I will release them. And I will repeat this process as many times and as often as necessary. Because I am worthy of and capable of forgiveness. And with this extension of grace to myself and others comes the power to move forward in confidence with my decision to become a more mindful, intentional consumer. I commit to doing so not only for myself, but also for the people and community I love. Now I move forward with renewed purpose and gratitude for the gift of forgiveness.

Asé,

Now that you have acknowledged that you have more than you need and are committed to the beautiful and important work of forgiveness, you have *finally* reached the mile marker on your journey I know that you've been waiting for: It's time to let go of what no longer serves you, to make space for what does.

Let's Recap:
The Forgiveness Process

- Forgiveness is an act of redemption and grace that we extend to ourselves and others who may have knowingly or unknowingly contributed to our lives of excess.
- Forgiveness is an opportunity to release any and all negative emotions that are the result of acknowledging that we have more than we need.
- Forgiveness is a gift, a way to free ourselves from the harmful behaviors of our past so that we can move forward with renewed hope and confidence on the journey to live with less.

step three

LET GO!

Congratulations on acknowledging and forgiving yourself for the many things that are now waiting for you to make a very important decision: what you want to keep and what you need to let go.

You are finally here, the point in your minimalist journey where you get to finally release what no longer serves you. But before you jump in, let me give you a fair warning: the process of letting go is not as easy as it might appear.

Certainly, there will be items that you are able to and more than willing to immediately let go. The clothing, shoes, and accessories that are no longer wearable because they are stained or outdated. The kitchen gadgets that are missing parts or rusted with age. The gifts that you hated but were too nice to be honest about in the moment. Those things are easy. I'm talking about letting go of the hard stuff, those things that you love or have formed attachments to that you don't need or never use. They're going to be hard to let go.

Most of your belongings are items that, at some point, you purchased and accepted into your life because you wanted them. As you now know, once you allowed these items to have a space in your home, you began to form attachments to them. That is why, all too often, we find it difficult to release items that no longer serve us and instead "set them aside" or put them away in storage with the belief that, even though they are not what we want right now, we *may* want them in the future. We set aspiration goals for these items such as hoping to wear an outfit again when we reach a desired weight, or we convince ourselves that we will need them for a special occasion in the future (for which we still have not received an invitation).

We also have difficulty letting go of certain items for sentimental reasons. And when we must, such as at a garage sale, we tend to price them at the value of what they mean to us instead of their actual value. Have you ever gone to a yard sale and come across a simple glass vase only to have the owner try to convince you why it's worth one hundred dollars and not ten? There's usually a sentimental reason attached that means nothing to you, and so you walk away without the vase and more than likely it goes back into the owner's home unless or until he's willing to acknowledge what it's actually worth. But more often than not, people refuse to let go of sentimental objects and instead find ways to try to make them work in their décor or put them away in storage—even though it's out of sight, you know that's it's still there, holding its sentimental value while remaining unused. Ah, it's safe, and that safety also helps you feel secure in knowing that you still own something that you love so much.

From forming attachments to our fears of loss aversion, we continue to hold on to things that serve no purpose for future use, sentimental reasons, or simply because we purchased them with our hard-earned money and cannot imagine giving them away for free or at a fraction of the cost.

Trust me, I understand. For me, letting go was a real struggle.

Letting Go: The Struggle

Following the only consistent advice I could find, after acknowledging that I had more than I needed and forgiving myself, I began the daunting task of sorting through items and placing them in designated piles: keep, donate, and trash. But as the organized piles grew larger, I realized I had no idea how much we truly owned. There was no way my journey to minimalism would start on Saturday morning and end by Sunday night. There was a lot to sort through.

And when I say a lot, I mean *a lot*.

Clothing with price tags still attached hung alongside outfits that no longer fit. Shoes that had long since walked their last walk were stacked between boxes of unworn pairs. Tarnishing jewelry. Scarves balled into Gordian knots. Conference swag T-shirts that were too hideous to even wear as pajamas. And in one rarely opened jewelry box, I discovered several old watches that were perfectly fine—they just needed new batteries.

Throughout the house were dozens of candles with unlit wicks. Bowls of potpourri that no longer held any fragrance.

123

Home goods still inside their original packaging, usually accompanied by a receipt with a ninety-day return policy that had long since expired. Every time I thought I had made progress I would find another handbag that I had hidden inside of a larger handbag and cry.

It was madness, a vicious cycle of trying to decide what to keep and what to let go, all while experiencing a range of emotions. Excitement upon discovering something I had thought was lost. Laughter whenever I found items that I knew I would never wear again (and was not quite sure why I had worn them in the first place). But without a doubt I experienced more negative emotions than positive.

Whenever I came across uncomfortable, designer stilettos, I sighed with shame. Heels had barely a scratch because I only ever wore them to walk from my car to the office, where I would take them off and leave them under my desk for the rest of the day. There was anger whenever I looked at the ever-growing donation and consignments piles. Disappointment as I mentally calculated all the money that I had spent and would never be able to recoup. Those heavy feelings of humiliation, frustration, embarrassment, and guilt that I had *just* forgiven myself for reemerged. And of course, there were once again lots and lots of tears.

How was I supposed to decide what to keep and what to let go among *all this stuff*? Even after I had decided what to keep, donate, and trash, the "keep" pile still contained a significant amount of things. I realized that if I truly wanted to live with less, I would have to follow a practical but difficult philosophy: I had to decide what among the items I not only loved but needed and would use.

FOR THE CULTURE
▼▲▼▲▼

It is important for people of the African diaspora and other marginalized communities to understand they may find the letting-go process especially challenging. Often, our loss aversion is rooted in the perceived power that comes with ownership, and it may be especially difficult to part with expensive wares or luxury items that have social currency.

Additionally, you may own things that have value beyond what others think they are worth due to their cultural or familial significance, and it is important to put them aside for future consideration. Examples of items that have personal significance and value include ancestral spiritual texts such as your great-grandmother's Bible, manumission papers, or your family's first deed to property. Note that even though you may not use these things, you need and love them because of what they represent in your life.

Need. Use. Love.

Applying the "need, use, love" philosophy to my belongings was the only way I was able to truly assess what items it was time to release from my life. Starting out, I thought "love" was the only feeling I needed. If I loved it, I placed an item in the "keep" pile. Unsurprisingly, it didn't whittle down the list all that much. But when I added the considerations of "need" and "use," I found myself asking time and time again: Do I *really* love this or am I holding on to it for some other reason?

The benefit of "need, use, love" is that it is all-encompassing, a way to objectively look at your belongings to determine whether they should remain in your life. Obviously, if we looked at these considerations individually, we would have a justification to keep everything we own. You may need something but not love it. You may love something but not use it. That's why every item you are considering has to meet all three criteria: You have to need, use, and love it . . . or let it go.

Determining Need

How do we know whether we actually need something? Well, you're going to have to be honest with yourself when it comes to what you truly need (and don't need) to live with less. Of course, this is also an exercise in self-awareness and discipline, so keep in mind that if you want to convince yourself that you need something, you probably will. That is why I want you to consider to the following rubric when it comes to determining need:

Time is your key indicator when it comes to need, because if you haven't needed the item recently, chances are pretty high you won't need it in the future, either.

Ask Yourself

When was the last time I needed this item?
If the item is part of your wardrobe, when was the last time you needed to wear it? If the item is a gadget or appliance, when was the last time you needed it to get the job done? If the item is part of a collection, when was the last time you needed to look, read, or hold it to bring you joy?

Determining Use

As with "need," time is one of the biggest factors to consider when it comes to whether you actually use an item. It's easy to think that you are going to use the lost thing you just rediscovered as a result of the acknowledgment process. But are you really going to use it when just a few hours before you didn't even know you had it? Again, this assessment will require you to be honest. And be careful to not base your decision on what I like to call "possibly, maybe, in the future" use. If you might use it, there's your answer: It's highly likely that you won't.

Ask Yourself

When was the last time I used this item?
If the item is part of your wardrobe, when was the last time you wore it? If it is a gadget or appliance, when was

the last time you used it to get the job done? If the item is part of a collection, when was the last time you used it to bring you joy?

Determining Love

Ah, love. One of the greatest extensions of ourselves. Unfortunately, when it comes to our belongings, love is often rooted in arbitrary factors and attachments. We love things because they are beautiful. We love things because of who made or gave them to us. We love things because of the status or prestige we feel simply by owning them. And for so many other reasons that are simply not enough to justify keeping things. You have to love your belongings enough to make space for them in your life. And sometimes, that makes the decision a little more difficult.

As it always is with matters of the heart, determining what you love is a deeply personal process. This is the last question for good reason—you should determine whether you need and use something before asking yourself if you love it. Because our love for our belongings can be fleeting, and you may even find yourself letting go of something later in your journey when your relationship to the item has changed.

If you need it, and you use it, and you love it (at least for now), then that's enough. There are no prizes for letting go of things you aren't ready to release—but be honest with yourself. "Love" isn't about what your mom loves, or your friend loves, or you-from-five-years-ago loved, or what you think you *should* love. Love is about honoring you, now, in this moment and giving yourself space to grow.

Ask Yourself

How much do I truly love this item?
If the item is part of your wardrobe, do you love it enough to make space for it? If the item is a gadget or appliance, do you love it enough to keep and make space for it by letting something else go? If the item is part of a collection, do you love it enough that if it's the only item that you get to keep, you will be satisfied and content with your decision?

As it always is with matters of the heart, determining which items you love enough to make space for won't always be easy. And you may find yourself either setting items aside for future consideration and assessment, or even letting them go later in your journey, when you are able to look at your affinity for them differently.

A Note About Kids

I am frequently asked how to involve children in the letting-go process. Given the statistics, many children have more than they need. But here's some news that might surprise you—young people don't have as much difficulty as adults with letting things go. When it comes to children and the letting-go process, it is about the approach. Rather than bursting into your child's room and declaring, "You have too much stuff! Clean this room and get rid of some of this stuff now!" try this approach instead:

> Calmly tell your child there are so many children who are less fortunate. Ask your child if he/she/ they would be willing to give away some clothing, books, and toys to make another child happy. Hand your child a donation bag and ask her/him/them to fill it. Then close the door and allow your child to go through the letting-go process on their own.

Not only is it likely that your child will fill the bag quickly, he/she/they may ask for another donation bag! And lastly, a word of caution: Do not look at your child's donations. What they have chosen to donate might actually hurt your feelings. You are likely to discover that many things they said they *had* to have are just that—things.

There were quite a few belongings that I struggled to part with during the letting-go process but there is one item that has become the story I share about my journey time and time again: my black Kasper power suit. I just couldn't let it go. Until I applied the "need, use, love" philosophy and established what would become the last stage in the letting-go process: finding a way to pay it forward by allowing it to serve someone else.

It is important to note this was not my only black power suit. I had several! But there was something about this Kasper suit that made it difficult to donate or consign. Yes, I had several black power suits but I needed this one because whenever I wore it, I felt like I could conquer the world. Sure, I had not worn it in a very long time but after trying and failing to write my second novel, I was facing the very real possibility that I would have to return to the corporate world and this would be the suit I'd wear to every interview. And did I love it? Ah, man, did I *love it*!

Simply looking at it hanging in my closet or holding it up to myself in the mirror reminded me how beautiful it was and how beautiful I looked when I wore it. The exquisite detailing. The gorgeous buttons. The perfect hem that rested at the perfect spot above my knees.

How could I let it go? How could I risk never again having an opportunity to wear the power suit I never wore? What about the possible job interviews when I would need to look and feel like I was ready to conquer the world?

This is the "make-or-break" moment that often occurs during the letting-go process. It's the stunning sweater that's too big. The designer pants that are too small. The kitchen gadget that you might to need to use if you ever decide to tackle making your grandma's infamous pound cake. Those items that you just can't seem to part with . . . even though they serve no purpose other than taking up space.

After whittling away at your belongings, you will undoubtedly be left with a few things that are difficult to let go based on their actual worth or their perceived value. It can be as simple as the kitchen gadget you hope or plan to use at a family gathering or as complicated as a designer piece that might be worth something because it's "this close" to being considered vintage.

You know you don't need these items. You know you will never use these items. But your affinity for them is so strong, you have found ways to justify them as meeting each element of the "need, use, love" approach just so you can keep them. When you inevitably reach this stage in the process, I want you to ask yourself one simple question.

Ask Yourself

How long am I going to continue to hold on to things that I don't need or use just because I don't want to let them go?

Letting Go: More Than Just a Tidy Home

Pia Thompson is the founder of Sweet Digs, a home organization company that helps people declutter using the KonMari Method. As a self-proclaimed Joy Finder, Pia knows that "letting go" is more than just having a tidy home. It's also an opportunity to curate your home and wardrobe with self-love and intention! Here are four of Pia's favorite tips to make letting go an act of self-care and self-love:

1. **Create an empowering "letting-go" environment.** Schedule your tasks for the time of day when you show up best.
2. **Expect the process to take twice as long.** Letting go can bring up deep emotions, and you want time to choose with intention.
3. **Don't keep anything that makes you feel bad about yourself.** Gain freedom to be yourself by letting go of anything that brings up a lack of self-worth.
4. **Remove what you've "let go" from your home ASAP.** Otherwise, these things may find their way back into your space!

We allow things into our lives for so many reasons, so it's only natural that we struggle to let them go for a number of reasons as well. Because we are hopeful. Because we are fearful. Because we want it to remain in our possession "just in case." The reality is, these things are not truly serving us because they have no purpose other than taking up space in our lives.

When you reach the "make-or-break" point in your minimalist journey, the decisions that you have to make won't be easy. But you must find a way to let go of those things that no longer serve you—no matter how amazingly wonderful they are or may be in the future—if you truly want to live with less. When I reached this point in my own journey, the way I overcame the fears and the loss aversion I was experiencing was by finding ways to release the items so they could stop taking up space in my life, and instead serve someone else who truly needed, would use, and would love them.

It's time to pay it forward.

Let's Recap: The Letting-Go Process

- Letting go is a crucial step on the journey to live with less, a privilege and opportunity to decide what we want to keep in our lives and what we need to let go.
- Letting go may be difficult at times but it is part of our commitment to minimalism, a way to ensure that our lives only contain what we need, use, and love.
- Letting go is liberating! It is a way to release items that are taking up space to make room for what matters most.

step four

PAY IT FORWARD

Can you believe it? After learning about the principles of minimalism and discovering why you had more than you needed, you have done the amazing work of acknowledging your excess, forgiven yourself, and followed the "need, use, love" philosophy to determine what you want you to keep in your life. You have completed the emotional and labor-intensive phase of deciding what to let go to make space for what truly matters. Now it's time to pay it forward with the things that no longer serve you so that they can benefit others.

It's easy to think you're "done" when you have identified what you're ready to let go. But we have my black Kasper to thank for the final part of the process. See, I knew I had to let that suit go. But one of the reasons it was so challenging was that I didn't know *where* it could or should go!

I felt it was too nice to donate to a local thrift store. And if I gave it to a friend, I was certain that I'd find a reason to borrow it and it would ultimately end up back in my possession. I also didn't want to consign it because the local consignment shop I used had a strict policy: If an item didn't sell within thirty days, they didn't return it to you—it went straight to a donation center. (This is actually a pretty brilliant policy and worked just fine for other items I'd consigned in the hope of recouping at least some of the money I'd spent over the years. It was completely fine for those items to be donated if they didn't sell because I certainly didn't want them back in my closet. But the thought of my black Kasper suit going to a donation center that I didn't choose? The horror!)

Ah, the minimalist innocence and shenanigans. Sometimes I reflect fondly on the beginning of my journey and smile at the Afrominimalist who was still so clearly emotionally attached to items that she'd committed to let go.

I share these truths with you because, of course, now, five years into my journey—to the month of the publication of this book, in fact—it would have been so easy for me to pass along that black Kasper suit to anyone who assured me they needed and would use and love it. But early on in your journey, these decisions can be much harder to make, mainly because you are still learning the power of intention when it comes to the practice of minimalism. That is why I developed the "Pay It Forward" process, your first lesson on the power of intentionality. Being intentional about what we choose to do with the items we let go is just as important as the letting-go process itself.

A Lesson in Intention

As we know, intention is one of the guiding principles to curating and maintaining your new lifestyle with less. It will inform your future purchases as well as what you choose to allow into your life to ensure that it aligns with your decision to live a minimalist lifestyle *your way*. Paying it forward is a lesson in intention, an opportunity for you to be purposeful and to plan to make sure that your belongings don't get added to an already overflowing landfill and instead end up with people and organizations who need them the most.

Need. Use. Love.

Let's revisit my black Kasper suit for a moment. You know, the one I knew I needed to let go of but couldn't until I found it a deserving home? It's the perfect example of how the "need, use, love" philosophy can help you make donations with intention.

First, I had to look beyond family, friends, and consignment shops to think about what woman really needed this suit. It was professional attire, which meant it could benefit organizations that focused on professional development or offered career services.

Next, I had to determine which of these organizations in my community could actually use this suit. Assuming that an organization's mission aligned with helping women with professional development and career services wasn't enough. Of the several organizations that I researched, almost of all of them listed the sizes of the womens wear they needed, and I would have been doing them a disservice by donating a suit they couldn't use.

Lastly, I had to decide which organization would love to receive my black Kasper suit. (Bonus: All charitable organizations love receiving your donations—as long as they can use them.) I also had to consider which organization I loved, where I would be honored to donate my favorite suit to support and further their important work.

After researching several organizations and learning about their needs, it was clear which one would be receiving my black Kasper suit: Dress for Success. Now whenever I think about the woman who received it (and I am honored), preparing to reestablish herself and build her career, I am honored to have helped that woman get a fresh start on her life. I love knowing that just maybe she wore that black Kasper suit to an interview feeling powerful and ready to conquer the world.

Look Online, Call Ahead

Being intentional about your donations means doing the research so you don't end up burdening organizations with items they don't need. Don't make assumptions based on the name of the organization or even its mission. Look online to see if any of your belongings can fulfill their most urgent requests and call ahead to ask about the best days and times to drop off your items if this information isn't listed on their website. I discovered the utility of doing a little extra research when looking to donate clothing and shoes. My first thought was women's and family shelters because

I knew that most victims of domestic violence leave with very little, usually whatever they were wearing the moment they made the bold and brave decision to leave their abusers. However, upon researching a local shelter, I discovered their current top priorities were not clothing and shoes but rather laundry detergent, toiletries, feminine hygiene products, diapers, baby formula, and school supplies. At the bottom of the list of priorities was clothing, and what they needed was winter attire in preparation for the upcoming season. My donations still wouldn't have been very helpful as they were summer attire.

Donations: Thinking Beyond Thrift Stores

I want you to apply the "need, use, love" framework to everything you are letting go. Doing so will be a powerful lesson on how to practice being intentional, and an opportunity to directly impact others in your community who are in need. And I'm not just talking about the usuals like the Salvation Army and Goodwill. These organizations do wonderful work, but there are likely dozens of other organizations within your own community where you can be impactful.

And don't be afraid to get creative! Think beyond thrift stores to fully harness the power of intention. There are organizations that need or will properly dispose of virtually every category of household items, from broken bicycles to building supplies and even old electronic equipment. Yes, it will require a little more sleuthing to find organizations that will benefit from your donations, but it is worth the extra effort—for the environment as well as the people you are seeking to help. Here are a few ideas to help you get started:

- **Charitable and Nonprofit Organizations**
  Research local charitable organizations that will give your donations directly to the people they serve or resell donations and use the profits to support their missions.

- **"Buy Nothing" and "No Waste" Groups**
  Research local "buy nothing" and "no waste" groups in your community and on social media, where you can post items that you wish to donate to a loving home.

- **Community Homes and Shelters**
  Research your local social service agencies to get a listing of local community homes and shelters so that you can learn about their immediate needs. Also, if you have the resources to do so, consider stopping by the store to purchase additional items that may be on their list of priorities because they are rarely donated, such as toiletries.

- **Recycling and Upcycling Programs**
  Research businesses, organizations, and manufacturers who will come pick up old appliances and other items with parts that can be used for recycling or upcycling. Many state and federal agencies have programs for appliances, such as the Environmental Protection Agency's Responsible Appliance Disposal program, a voluntary partnership program that works with utilities, retailers,

manufacturers, state and local government organizations, affiliates, and others to dispose of old refrigeration appliances using the best environmental practices available.

- **Community Kitchens and Pantries**
  Research food justice organizations in your community. Many are in need of kitchen appliances, cookware, dishes, and other kitchenware to service at-risk populations and children and families in need.

One of the best ways to pay it forward is to be intentional about deciding which individual, charitable organization, or social group should receive your donations. How will your donation support their target population and needs? Is this group willing to accept and find ways to reuse items that are generally trashed? Even if you ultimately end up taking your donations to a globally recognized thrift store, consider driving outside of your zip code if it will benefit a more marginalized community. Likewise consider donating to and partnering with organizations whose missions are aligned with initiatives that you support so that you are being intentional about your impact as well.

Let's Recap:
The "Pay It Forward" Process

- Paying it forward is an opportunity to release the things that no longer serve you so that they can benefit others in need.

- Paying it forward is a lesson in intention, a way for you to ensure that your donations go to the people and organizations who need and will use them.
- Paying it forward is a way to responsibly release the items that no longer serve you, by making sure they don't cause environmental harm or burden organizations with items that are not priorities and will not be useful.

part three

THE PRACTICE

Many people believe that "letting go" is the most challenging aspect of transitioning to a minimalist lifestyle. Without a doubt, acknowledging our overconsumption, trying to forgive ourselves, and determining what we need, use, and love versus what we should release can certainly *feel* like the most challenging work at times. But now that you have sorted through your belongings and let go of what no longer serves you, I want to share an exciting truth: Your journey as a minimalist has only just begun.

But before we begin the work of exploring how to maintain and nurture what you have accomplished, please take a moment to congratulate yourself on making it to this stage. You have done the educational work of learning about the principles of minimalism as well as how the psychology of ownership can influence our choices as consumers. You have also done the emotional work of understanding and acknowledging why you have more than you need and have forgiven yourself and others who may have contributed, knowingly or unknowingly, to your former life of overconsumption. And of course, you have done the physical labor of discovering what you truly need, use, and love, and you have paid it forward by ensuring that others benefit from the items you have released. All of this takes courage, fortitude, and a strong sense of self.

Again, congratulations. You have given yourself a wonderful gift.

Now it is time to commit to the practice of maintaining your new lifestyle of less. And please know that you can and *will* do so successfully.

Trust me, you are more than adequately prepared for the journey to live with less as you continue to become a more intentional, mindful consumer. But remember, there is no destination (and this is part of the joy!). Maintaining a minimalist lifestyle will require you to continuously let go of what no longer serves you to make space for what matters.

"Your journey as a minimalist is an opportunity for you to embrace the freedom to do and have more of what matters by being authentic and intentional with what you accept and allow to remain in your life."

—Christine

Authenticity. Intention. These are two important principles to chart your path. Throughout your journey to live with less, you will make many beautiful discoveries. Allowing authenticity and intention to guide and dictate your practice will ultimately result in you receiving the greatest reward: freedom. Although the work will not be easy at times, being a minimalist can lead to you becoming the best version of yourself. As you continue to discover the benefits of living with less, authenticity and intention will become easier and, in time, an essential part of your everyday life. Like any muscle that is being developed, consistently making decisions that are rooted in these principles will strengthen your ability to ensure your life is composed of only what you need, use, and love.

So, let us continue to expand on your important work by defining and establishing personal rules and mantras that will ensure you have and can maintain a minimalist lifestyle that aligns with your needs and goals.

the power of authenticity

I believe authenticity is instinctive, that it is our innate sense of being. It resonates in our hearts. It nestles in our souls. It settles in our bones. When we are being guided by authenticity, the choices we make just feel right.

The lesson of authenticity remains one of my most joyful and unintended discoveries throughout my minimalist journey. From incorporating an Afrocentric home aesthetic to creating a nontraditional, colorful capsule wardrobe, I make authentic choices and remain honest about aspects of mainstream minimalism that simply do not work for me. As the elders in my community often advise, "Take a little. Leave a little."

There are many unofficial rules when it comes to the practice of minimalism, but I have learned that even some of the guidance from respected practitioners may not work for my lifestyle. So, I take what works and I depart from what doesn't. And through this continuous process of self-discovery, I have learned the power of authenticity—it is the only way to ensure I can have and maintain a minimalist lifestyle that works for me.

Authenticity informs what I allow into my life and what I release. It even guides what content I share with the online minimalist community and in workshops. After all, being genuine in my approach to living with less is how I became the Afrominimalist. Who knows what my life would look and feel like if I had not been honest and authentic throughout this process?

It goes without saying that I would not have created a life of less that is rooted in my love and appreciation for Black history and culture. It also goes without saying that I would not be as happy and content with my home, wardrobe, and related lifestyle choices. That is why I believe that anyone who wants to live with less must tap into the power of authenticity to not only create their minimalist lifestyle but also to maintain it.

This is *your* life. Therefore, your home's aesthetic as well as your wardrobe and other personal effects should reflect what brings *you* joy. Of course, you can and should still look to others for inspiration. The minimalist community is composed of wonderful people who enjoy sharing their insights and solutions for small-space living. Your fellow minimalists can provide a wealth of resources and be a source of encouragement. Being authentic in your practice simply means being mindful, that you avoid mirroring someone else's lifestyle or what you *think* minimalism should look and feel like.

One of the best ways to tap into your authenticity is to reflect on what remains after completing the "letting-go" process. Surely, many of your decisions regarding what to keep and what to let go were not easy. However, in addition to decluttering and shedding excess, the "letting-go" process served another important purpose as you began to define your personal practice: It made you more aware of what brings you joy—you just needed to let go of some things to see it!

As you begin curating your minimalist lifestyle with authenticity, you will continue to discover what you need to be content with less. And I encourage you to embrace your uniqueness as an individual. No one knows you better than you. Each discovery of determining what you need, use, and love will not only inform your home design and wardrobe, but it will also influence your decisions to acquire new things as well as whether to accept or respectfully decline gifts, free swag, and other items from well-meaning people. Learning to say, "This does not serve me," requires you to be honest and disciplined, and you will have to commit to this truth time and time again.

> "Authenticity is a core aspect of taking back your power as a consumer."
>
> —Christine

Now that your rose-colored glasses are off, you understand the psychology of ownership and why you once had more than you needed. Authenticity adds an extra layer of protection to deciding what to keep and allow into your life. Once you embrace your true self and know what genuinely brings you joy, it is much harder to be enticed by things that do not align with your lifestyle. Authenticity is one of your superpowers as a consumer. Soon it will become much easier to see a beautiful item for what it really is—simply another beautiful thing, rather than something you must purchase or accept.

Embracing your authenticity is one sure way to welcome and allow into your life only those things that you truly need, use, and love.

Need. Use. Love.

To ensure that authenticity remains at the forefront of your minimalist practice, regularly assess your belongings as well as intended purchases and gifts by asking yourself three questions:

1. Do I need this, or will I need this soon?
2. Will I use this, or will I use this soon?
3. Do I love this, or will I come to love this soon?

If the answer to any of these questions is no, pay it forward by letting the item go, forgo purchasing the item, or respectfully decline whatever is being offered to you.

Although I discovered the power of authenticity by trial and error, there are ways to be guided strategically by your own definition of authenticity and cultivate your minimalist lifestyle. Remember, you have already started this discovery through the process of letting go. Releasing items that you no longer need, use, and love helped you better understand and recognize what you do! Now you can truly see what matters most . . . to you!

Curating Your Home: Authenticity over Aesthetics

Even amid clutter, our living spaces hold the best clues to our most authentic selves. No matter how small or large the residence, your home contains items you value enough to give them a place in one of your most sacred spaces. After parting ways with the unnecessary among your belongings, what remains are the most authentic reflections of what you value and need to sustain you.

Note the reasons why you find these items significant and important enough to remain in your home. What are the reasons you decided to keep certain belongings and not others? What parts of you do these things speak to, and what purposes do they fulfill? Allow these observations to serve as beacons as you continue to discover and curate an authentic, minimalist décor.

One way to do this is by using a modified version of the "need, use, love" philosophy. As you assess your belongings, ask yourself:

1. What do I need to make my home feel authentic?
2. How can I use my living spaces to reflect my authenticity?
3. How can I ensure that my home is a reflection of what I love?

This framework can assist in your process of creating an authentic minimalist aesthetic that represents who you are and what brings you joy.

The Sanctuary You Need

Beyond our essentials and necessities, we all have additional things in our living spaces that we need to make our homes feel like home. For me, this includes items that reflect the beauty of the African diaspora, such as reupholstered furnishings in colorful Ankara prints and play-
ful patterns, cultural items acquired from my travels, and historical and literary texts on the Black experience. And of course, there is the mason jar filled with raw cotton that reminds me to thank and honor my ancestors' fortitude and resilience.

These items are not only aspects of my home's décor; they are also representatives of my life's work and my most authentic self—a Black woman who loves the African diaspora and has dedicated her life to preserving and teaching its rich history. I continue to use my love for the African diaspora to determine what I need to make my minimalist home feel intentional and purposeful. As a result, my home feels like more than a place of shelter. Home is my sanctuary.

Knowing that Afro-inspired wares are a part of my home's authenticity has not only helped me curate my living space with intention, but it has also served as a guideline for what home goods I purchase as well as what items I allow into my sacred space. But what does that look like in practice? It means:

- Being a mindful consumer by only purchasing and accepting items that represent what is important to me and align with my Afrominimalist aesthetic.
- Deciding which aspects of my professional life I want to see regularly that can serve as reminders to keep me focused and engaged in my work.
- Determining which family heirlooms and cultural mementos I display to ground and sustain Black womanhood.

Among my home goods is one item that is equally as infamous as my orange jumpsuit: a beautiful coffee cup with a gold handle that is hand-painted with an Afrocentric motif. Of course, rarely does one need a new coffee cup (in fact, I have a conspiracy theory that mugs multiply and fill our cupboards without any action on our part!). However, as soon as I saw this cup (which was clearly made for *the* Afrominimalist), I knew that I needed to add it to my collection. Elegant and cultural, it embodied my minimalist aesthetic *and* checked all the boxes for why I allow new items into my life.

I use this beautiful coffee cup almost daily, and whenever I do, I feel like quite the queen as I joyfully savor my beverage. I also photograph this cup often, and much like my orange jumpsuit, it has become representative of my Afrominimalist persona. If you need and want to use a mug to drink coffee, why not have one that represents your authentic self and brings you joy? Purchasing this cup also served another purpose—I made space for it by donating mugs I rarely used to a local coworking facility.

FOR THE CULTURE

▼▲▼▲▼

People of the African diaspora and other marginalized groups often have items of cultural significance that are more than decoration—they are grounding and essential to our survival, both symbolic and sacred. We need them even though they may not align perfectly with the "need, use, love" philosophy.

While mainstream minimalism might question my decision to have two religious texts and suggest that I part with one, only I know the value of both. There is the religious text that I use for personal study, which is different from the religious text that belonged to my great-grandmother. The latter is sacred, something that I can hold when I need to be encouraged and reassured of my foremother's fortitude by carefully looking at the highlighted words that grounded and anchored her through difficult moments. I *need* both.

As you incorporate the "need, use, love" philosophy into your personal practice, remember to honor not only your authenticity but also your ancestry. Both can be very influential in determining what you keep and allow as you curate your home with intention.

Throughout my minimalist journey, I have repeated this process in some form or fashion many times. Once I discovered the minimalist aesthetic I wanted in my home, I slowly began welcoming in home goods and décor that represented Afrominimalism and are an authentic representation of my life with less. And of course, I continued to release items that no longer had a place so they could serve others. Over time, my home has come to represent the Afrocentric minimalist aesthetic that many people have come to admire. But mostly, that *I* admire.

Reimagining Your Space

Discovering what décor your home needs to feel authentic is both liberating and energizing. You realize you are truly curating one of the most sacred personal spaces in your life. It is the beginning of reimagining your home as more than a residence, more than a piece of property that you rent or own. Through this reimagining, home becomes the sanctuary and haven that we all need and deserve.

But your reimagining should not end with décor. It should extend to every inch of square footage as you continue to cultivate your minimalist practice with intention.

Just as it is with discovering your personal aesthetic, authenticity can serve as a guide for looking beyond traditional and mainstream layouts to use your living space in ways that work best for you. There are artists who have converted their living rooms into studios and, instead, use their spare bedrooms for gathering and lounging. Some homeschool educators forgo their family's basement as an additional area to lounge and, instead, utilize the space for teaching and learning. In my home, with the flip of a tabletop or the repositioning of functional, easy-to-move furniture, my living room serves as a multipurpose space—from working and dining to movie nights and even slumber parties for my teenager and her friends. (Almost as infamous as my orange jumpsuit and favorite Afrocentric coffee mug are the two IKEA chaises in my multipurpose space. Pushed together, these chaises serve as a glorious, spacious couch. Separately, they serve as single beds for guests!)

Reimagine the rooms in your home as opportunities to reflect not only your authentic style, but also your unique and authentic life. Do you have rooms that are furnished but rarely used? Do you occupy spaces based on their expected use instead of using a different area that would be more functional? Home is a living space that can be reimagined and reconfigured to best suit the needs of your household.

If you are unsure which rooms in your home are underutilized, consider researching government and local organizations that provide free heat map imaging to track your movements. (Trust me, it is not as scary and invasive as it might sound.) Reviewing the results of your property might surprise you. After heat-mapping our marital home, I discovered we barely used much of the 2,500-plus-square-foot living space. Most of our time was spent in our respective bedrooms and the eat-in kitchen despite having a generous living room, formal dining room, and family room in the basement. It was one of the reasons I was certain we could live in a smaller home!

If downsizing is not an option, consider ways to reimagine your home to authentically live a meaningful and intentional minimalist life. Think beyond the traditional! An unused or rarely used guest bedroom can serve multiple purposes that are more aligned with your new lifestyle. (Indoor botanical garden, anyone?)

Nix the Neutrals

As you continue to tap into the power of authenticity, also continue to reimagine your home's interior design. Because of the popularity of mainstream minimalism, many people believe there is only one way that minimalism can "look," but the barren, neutral aesthetic is not for everyone. It most certainly was not for me.

One of the reasons I chose to embrace minimalism was that I was drawn to the simplicity represented in popular media. But instead of making my home feel cozy, my living spaces felt sterile, almost institutional. My living room lacked vibrant hues that make my home feel warm and welcoming. Throughout my living space, the beautiful, varied textures were lost amid the monochrome arrangements.

The end result? I hated it.

While looking at pictures of minimalist spaces can be helpful and even inspiring, I caution against making them your goal. In addition to many minimalist furnishings being costly and inaccessible, you run the risk of finding yourself in either of two precarious situations: (1) being unable to mirror a certain aesthetic, which may make you feel discouraged and lead you to believe there is no way that you can obtain a minimalist lifestyle, or (2) spending resources mimicking an aesthetic only to discover it just does not feel like you. As someone who often retreats to the bedroom as a sanctuary, I found myself desolate and longing for the luxurious feeling of calming, soothing color palettes. And as I slowly learned to embrace what felt authentic, I've been able to design rooms and spaces that felt like home to me.

I repurposed many of the neutral home goods I invested in through using sustainable solutions such as upholstery. I learned to tap into the power of a multifunctional living space and, in time, curate each aspect of my home's design (it took five years!).

Ask Yourself

1. During the "letting-go" process, what items did I decide to keep because I need, use, and love them? What aspects of these belongings reflect my authenticity?

2. What items were easy for me to part with? Why was I initially drawn to them? (This self-reflection will help you curb your habit of purchasing and accepting items that you do not need, use, and love!)

3. What textures, patterns, and textiles bring me joy? What about these design elements motivates me? What color palettes make me feel calm and serene? What color palettes make my home feel warm and welcoming?

4. What items and mementos do I cherish and why? How can I welcome more meaningful things into my life, and am I willing to release items to make space for them?

5. Which of my spaces and home furnishings do I need to reimagine and/or repurpose so they align with my authentic, minimalist goals?

Knowing the answers to these questions will help you make informed decisions about what to keep and allow into your home to ensure your choices and resulting aesthetic reflect authenticity.

I highly recommend adhering to the guidance of tiny home dwellers: Live in your space awhile before purchasing and acquiring more things. Spend some time reflecting on your current belongings to remember why you purchased or chose to inherit them. If you are unhappy with some of your furnishings and home goods, consider sustainable ways to repurpose them, such as repainting and upholstery. If you are unable or unwilling to donate some of your larger pieces, consider selling them or bartering with someone in your community for something more aligned with what you desire. There is no shame in having unfinished and undecorated spaces as you curate your minimalist life with authenticity and intention.

Don't rush! The practice of minimalism is a lifestyle, not a destination. Living with less is a lifelong commitment, so take the time you need to create a minimalist home that is an authentic reflection of you. Living with less requires constant discipline, which is often an act of individual accountability. Remember, being a mindful consumer means only allowing things into your life that you will need, use, and love. And what these things are can and *will* change from moment to moment, season to season. Like many other areas in our lives, your minimalist practice will always be a work in progress.

Just Say "No" to Storage

Unless you are truly fortunate, chances are pretty high that you'll end up moving residences more than once in your lifetime. And while storage units can be useful for local and in-state storage, I discourage con-  sidering such facilities as a solution for your out-of-state needs. The farther you move away from the things you once owned, the less likely it is that you'll come back for them. Trust me, I know this scenario well; storage units were my go-to moving solution before embracing minimalism!

The thing is, even if you eventually go back for those belongings, you'll have to keep paying the storage rental fees or risk the company taking legal action, including selling your belongings (hello, *Storage Wars*). Also, bear in mind that rarely does life go as planned: Even when you are well-meaning and intent on returning, you never know what may cause a costly delay. I'd planned to tackle my last storage facility in 2020—a unit in Florida that I acquired after graduating from law school—but an unexpected global pandemic ensured that I'd have to continue to pay for that couch and matching toddler chair that were just too cute to part with back in 2007. How quickly does time pass (and do rental fees add up)? The toddler who once sat in that chair is currently filling out applications for college!

There is no one way to live with less. Let me say that again. There is no one way to be a minimalist. Just as you do not have to own a certain number of things to practice minimalism, the things that you do own do not have to be restricted to a certain color palette or mirror a particular aesthetic. Tap into the power of authenticity to create unique living spaces that you will enjoy and cherish for years to come. And remember to have fun and enjoy the journey!

Words of Wisdom: Nicole Crowder

Nicole Crowder is a master upholsterer whose work has appeared in popular retail spaces like West Elm and on the pages of Martha Stewart Living. What makes Nicole's work special is her ability to help others reimagine family heirlooms that are often unused but difficult to part with. Nicole helps others realize upholstery as a sustainable solution to redesign items that are loved so they will be needed and used for years to come.

There is much peace in salvaging the bones of old furniture, of rubbing orange oil into the curves of a dried frame and watching a piece reveal itself to me. But beyond the beauty of restoring a piece, my desire to reupholster furniture is an extension of my belief in healthy ecosystems and sustainability.

I think a lot about furniture because items are rarely recycled, which results in over nine million tons of household waste annually. I myself have moved many apart- ments in many cities, and a few years ago I realized what I wasn't  carrying forward to each new place was my story. I did not have any heirloom pieces, nor did I have many items I felt attached to. I always gifted my furniture and sundry belongings to friends, family, and strangers, keeping a few items here and there. But I began interrogating my own rationale for wanting to constantly "start fresh." Why was I so unattached to things and willing to let them go instead of reimagining them in my next space? That questioning shifted the way I approach my work, which I pivoted to fo- cus on furniture with intentional designs that would hope- fully become part of someone else's heirloom history.

The next time you think about purchasing new fur- niture, consider whether your family and friends have pieces they no longer use but have been unwilling to part with for sentimental reasons. Perhaps, rather than ending up in a landfill, these pieces can be reimagined, reuphol- stered, and rehomed with love. And the next time you plan on discarding furniture, pause and ask yourself, "Can this possibly serve someone else?" Perhaps, all it needs is someone like me to peacefully salvage its old bones, rub a little orange oil into the curves of its dried wooden frame before upholstering it in a new fabric. Perhaps, actually I am certain, much the furniture we so easily discard can be passed on to a new home where it is needed, will be used, and most certainly loved.

Home: A Reflection of What You Love

One of the easiest considerations in the "need, use, love" philosophy is love. But is it really that easy? During the "letting-go" process you undoubtedly discovered many items that you loved . . . but did not need and use. It is the reason you must address all three considerations when deciding what to keep and allow into your home. Otherwise, there would be few items for you to part with. One of the reasons we have things is that we loved them, whether in the moment or for an extended period.

So, how can you ensure that your home reflects what you love? By tapping into the power of authenticity.

When it comes our homes, love is a necessity. Much like authenticity, it is an extension and offering of our innate sense of being. Love, too, resonates in our hearts. It nestles in our souls. It settles in our bones. When we are being guided by love, the choices we make also just feel right.

Of course, we regularly assess and declare our love for living beings. Without a doubt, we know when we have developed a deep affection for our family, friends, and pets (and plants!). But how do we discover and acknowledge this same affinity for our possessions? How can we be certain our love is not a momentary attraction to something simply because it is beautiful or has sentimental value? How do we know our love for a particular item is the real thing and not the result of an attachment?

I will be honest. Just as it can be with romantic relationships, the love we have for our possessions is complicated.

After I completed the "letting-go" process, I was certain that I needed, used, and loved everything that remained, especially because I took the "slow and steady" approach. But month after month, I found myself still letting go of items. As my authentic approach to minimalism continued to evolve, I had to acknowledge an uncomfortable truth: I'd kept quite a few things because of their perceived or actual worth and others simply because I just wasn't quite ready to part with them.

Among these items was a beautiful dining room table from a high-end retailer that I had purchased for a fraction of the cost from its previous owner. With a large round glass top that sat on an ebony wooden base with clean lines, the table was truly a statement piece. The problem? It was an investment I had made for our marital property, where it fit the large eat-in kitchen perfectly. But I loved this dining table so much, I was determined to make it work in my new, smaller living space.

It didn't.

Still, I tried.

First, I attempted to use the dining table in my multipurpose living room. But the piece was too large, and I constantly bumped into it. And there was no denying it made the already small space feel smaller.

Still, I tried.

As my writing career continued to blossom, I decided to use

the dining table as a desk—first, in the multipurpose living room and later in my bedroom (which is even smaller than the living room). While the dining table provided ample writing space, it was too bulky. Due to the size and shape of the glass top, there were few options for placement, no way for me to push it against one of the four corners. As a result, it made my bedroom feel cluttered and cumbersome to navigate.

Still, I tried.

For nearly four years, I tried to make the dining room table function in a living space that was almost five times smaller than the home I had purchased it for. That is how much I loved this table! Until one day, I finally acknowledged that it just did not and would never work in my new home . . . and I let it go.

Instantly, our multipurpose living room felt larger. Without the constant need to design around a piece of furniture with such a large footprint, I was able to see the possibilities of the room more clearly. I rearranged my other furnishings to make the space even more functional. Releasing that dining room table that I loved (but which obviously did not fit my minimalist home) was so liberating! And it didn't take long for me to find a new (smaller) dining table that is better suited to my family's needs.

Learning to Love and Let Go

Throughout your minimalist journey, you will have to be honest about why you love certain items and whether they truly serve your lifestyle of less. And this will likely take time. Some things we love are just harder to let go of than others, especially items that are still in great condition, and still beautiful, still valuable. But ensuring your home reflects your authenticity requires you to let go of items that you love that, unfortunately, are simply unable to serve your needs.

Rather than try to sell the dining room table or donate it to a thrift store, I took it to an area in my community where people often leave beloved items in the hopes that a fellow neighbor can use them. When I checked an hour later, it was gone. And I love knowing that the dining room table that I cherished so much went to another loving home.

Honesty is the core of authenticity. Even though it may be difficult, the time may come (actually, I *know* it will come) when you have to part with things that you love to create the minimalist home you desire.

"Don't be afraid to love and let go."

—Christine

Whatever items do not align with your authentic self and the aesthetic you desire, part ways with them and allow them to serve someone else. Yes, even some of the things you love. *Especially* some of the things you love. By doing so, you will continue to make space for things in your life that matter and support your minimalist practice.

Ask Yourself

1. Why do I love this item?
2. Does this item represent and/or reflect the minimalist practice I am creating?

3. Am I holding on to this item because it has actual value, perceived value, or sentimental value that makes it difficult for me to let go?
4. Do I know someone who can use this item who will love it? Do I have a way to part with this item so it can serve others?

Surely, the "need, use, love" philosophy is not the only way to create an authentic lifestyle with less. However, I believe it is a great way to begin the self-discovery of making your home décor and interior design feel authentic as well as determining how you can use your living spaces. Your ability to tap into the power of authenticity will only strengthen as you continue your journey to living with less. And it is my hope that you find this journey both joyful and liberating as you curate your home with authenticity and intention.

Words of Wisdom: Chanae Richards

Chanae Richards, interior designer and founder of Olorio Interiors, has an affinity for helping people curate their homes with authenticity and intention, especially when it comes to minimalist spaces. Her approach is simple: Home should not only represent how you feel your best, it should be where you feel your best.

I know what you're thinking—You've signed a lease. You've created Pinterest boards for Every. Single. Room.

Now, with your new keys in hand, you're asking, "What do I buy first?"

The answer: nothing.

Not one thing.

Yes, you will need something to sleep on. Got a blow-up bed? It is time to put it to use.

Live in your space first. Do not immediately buy that tufted California king you saw in your faves feed. Don't do it. And yes, this may mean camping out on an inflatable mattress for a few weeks. And if you're worried about what people will think, stop that. No seriously, stop. Real friends will bring takeout and eat with you on a radiator cover. Trust me. Get out of your head and really live in your new home.

By feeling your space out, your new home will tell you exactly what it needs. Will that entryway be better suited with a bench, console, or slim profile table? You'll walk in your front door for the seventh time and realize you *really* need a place to sit when taking your shoes off. Be patient. Be intentional.

In our personal living spaces, there is an alchemy that occurs between the very first time we walk into a new home and see the bare walls and the time we "feel it." And by "it," I mean a sense of comfort. A sense of freedom. A sense of belonging and knowing that we are home.

Home is more than a place to gather or eat meals during the day and a place to sleep at night. Yes, the doors, fixtures, and furnishings are all important elements to protect and comfort us. Don't rush.

a lesson in intention

Along with authenticity, intention is one of the most grounding and guiding principles in my minimalist practice, and over time, it has found its way into every area of my life. It informs my decisions, dictates my moves, and determines the words I speak and write. If I am a passenger on this wild ride called life, intention is the driver. And I have learned to wholeheartedly allow it to guide me.

But I was not always this way.

We all want to believe that we can be purposeful, that we are able to stick with our plans and not allow ourselves to be swayed. But often, when we see something that we want, it is easy to justify why we should have it. Very quickly, our determination to be intentional can transition to "I have to have this." That is why, much like authenticity, learning to be intentional is a lesson in self-discovery and discipline.

Fear is often a driving factor when it comes to determining what we need in our lives, which is why intention can so quickly find itself taking the backseat. Whether our fears stem from making sure we have enough food and toilet paper to survive an apocalypse or from making sure our homes are adequately furnished to meet cultural and societal expectations, if not managed, our fears can overtake our intentions. Before we know it, we can find ourselves once again engaged in overconsumption.

So how does one learn to be intentional, especially when fears and longings regularly show up in our everyday lives? It begins with first knowing what you want to achieve and then making a plan that includes ways to avoid going off course and how to course correct if you do. For me, this plan includes personal mantras and processes for those times I know I will be prone to emotional spending or find myself coming upon a deal so good, it would be criminal to leave it behind. Trusting yourself to be intentional in the moment is simply unrealistic. You must prepare for the inevitable: You will be tempted.

How many times have you visited a retail or grocery store for a few items, only to find yourself at the register with a shopping cart full of things? (Especially a red shopping cart that, let's say, has a white bull's-eye on it? Just me? Okay!) Have you ever come across beautiful furnishings or home goods only to purchase them and discover they do not fit your living space or aesthetic? You went shopping with good intentions; you may have even had a list! But in the moment, you were unable to follow through.

This is why you must find ways to remember your intention and commitment to live with less.

Remember to Pause

As someone who once prided herself on being a bargain shopper, I found that learning to pause was truly an arduous exercise in restraint. Pausing meant running the risk of someone else getting the deal! But learning to wait before making purchases has become integral to my lifestyle with less. This simple act has and continues to stop me from making unnecessary purchases or accepting things that I do not need and will not use. Notice that I refused to consider the "love" aspect here. When it comes to being intentional, love is the last consideration. Falling in love with an item is usually the reason we want to acquire it in the first place.

Reset Your Intentions

Before purchasing or accepting something that is unplanned for, take a minute to pause. During those sixty seconds, consider the reasons why you should allow this item to take up space in your life. Ask yourself questions to help realign your intentions:

1. Why do I feel like I need this item?
2. Does this item align with the goals and aesthetic I have set for my lifestyle with less?
3. If I need this item, is it something that I need right now?
4. Is this something that I can afford, monetarily and to take up space?

> The simple act of pausing to consider whether you should allow something into your life is one of the most effective strategies to be more mindful with what you keep and allow into your life. Within one minute, you can reset your intentions and determine whether you need an item, want an item, or were simply caught up in its beauty or the idea of getting a deal.

Have a Mantra

When pausing to reset your intentions, also keep in mind your self-reflections on why you once had more than you needed. For me, that means remembering my affinity for scoring a deal. Despite practicing minimalism for five years, I am still tempted at the sight of clearance signs, and when I inevitably find myself at the sales rack to "take a peek," my deal-finding skills are activated. Without fail, I am going to come upon something amazing, a deal too good to be true. That is why I find personal mantras helpful in remembering and resetting my intentions.

"Remember, it's not a deal if you don't need it."

—Christine

I have several mantras whenever I find myself at the sales rack or preparing to make a purchase. But without a doubt, my favorite and most effective speaks directly to the reason why I once had more than I needed: "Remember, it's not a deal if you don't need it!"

Surely, there have been salespeople concerned about my sanity as I either groaned or laughed out loud at the truthfulness of my personal shopping mantra. Because the reality is, if I purchase something I will not need or use, am I *really* getting a deal? If I purchase something for $25 that was originally $100, am I really saving $75? Or am I wasting $25? Regardless of my emotional reaction, saying, "Remember, it's not a deal if you don't need it," causes me to *take* action—I remember my intentions to live with less and put the item back.

Learning to pause and creating personal mantras will help you be more intentional about maintaining your minimalist lifestyle. Additionally, consider taking advantage of retailers' programs and services that can help you resist temptation. Instead of going to your favorite retail or grocery store to pick up a few items, consider ordering what you need online for curbside pickup to avoid the temptation of seeing items you didn't intend to buy.

Developing a reminder that speaks directly to the areas where you are prone to get off track will help you reset your intentions whenever you need to. Of course, you are more than welcome to use my favorite mantra. But I also encourage you to have fun creating your own!

But What About Gifts?

Whether it is due to holidays, annual birthday celebrations, or congratulatory milestones, there will inevitably come a time when you are offered or gifted an item that you don't want. When it comes to receiving gifts, I have found it easier to not accept these items rather than bring them into my life. Because when they come with home with me, I feel responsible and obligated to *try* to use and enjoy them.

"I really appreciate the kind gesture."

"This item is so beautiful, but I have to be honest, I really don't have the space for this."

"What a thoughtful gift! Unfortunately, I must be honest, I know that I really will not use this item."

(Bonus language: "I am really trying to be intentional about what to bring into my space. As you know, I am on a journey to live with less.")

However you choose to word it, you must be honest with the gift giver—no matter how well-meaning their offer. Learning to respectfully decline items is a superpower that you will have to exercise time and time again. And the free conference swag? Free gifts with purchase? All the freebies you will undoubtedly be offered that you really don't want? Just say, "No."

Gift with Care

Since we have all been on the receiving end of gifts that we don't need, use, or love, why not pay it forward by being mindful and intentional about the items *you* gift! I have two criteria when it comes to giving to others: either the items must be (1) charitable, such as donating to an important cause in the giftee's honor, or (2) it has to disappear (who doesn't love receiving treats like cookies or meals for a week, luxury bath soaps, and candles!)

One of the most meaningful gifts I ever received came via email: a notification that a friend had gifted a cow in my honor through Heifer International. It meant so much to know that this thoughtful gift would help end hunger and poverty for a community in need.

And don't be afraid to get kids in on the fun! Of all my daughter's birthday parties, the one she reflects on the most fondly is her eighth birthday. I was just at the beginning of my minimalist journey, and I knew the last thing she needed was more toys. Instead, we held a birthday carnival in our backyard. The cost of admission? In lieu of a gift, her guests had to bring one canned good to donate to our local food pantry. I'll never forget the texts I received from parents, like "Oh my goodness! My kid is raiding the pantry!"

We received bags of food donations and the kids all signed a card expressing their appreciation for the food pantry. The looks of surprise on the volunteers' faces when we showed up to make our donation! There were hugs, a tour of the food pantry, and many expressions of thanks. My daughter was so proud! (And yes, of course, I cried.)

When it comes to gifts, there are many ways to show people that you appreciate them without buying them things. Remember to gift with care!

I want to share another exciting truth with you: Not only has your journey as a minimalist only just begun, so has your journey to living with intention.

It is impossible to be intentional with only one aspect of your life.

Once I had my home under control, I noticed other areas of my life where I needed to be more intentional. From the writing projects I chose to accept to how I managed my time, intentionality has found its way into every aspect of my life. And I am so grateful!

Of course, learning to be intentional does not mean that all your challenges with acquiring things will go away. Confession: I still struggle with purchasing new notebooks and journals. (Early in my writing journey, I had convinced myself that my characters only wanted me to write in Rifle Paper Co. notebooks. Ha!)

Much like monthly "no spend" challenges, one way to be intentional about your purchases is to put yourself on a moratorium. Living with intention means you must consistently be honest with yourself *and* hold yourself accountable. Do you really need something to complete your assignments or fulfill your hobbies, or do you just want something new? To this day, I must exercise a "no new notebooks until you use the ones you have" rule. And there is no greater joy than getting to the last page of a notebook and knowing that I actually *need* to buy another one.

Guess What? Minimalists Buy Things!

One of the biggest misconceptions about minimalists is that we do not buy things. In reality, minimalists buy things all the time! Okay, not *all* the time and certainly not as much as we used to. But we certainly do purchase items. There is just one major difference: We are very intentional about what we buy and allow into the minimalist space we took great care to curate. Being a minimalist does not mean that you can no longer buy things, or even that you cannot *enjoy* buying things. Minimalists know that buying things is not what brings happiness. Rather, being intentional about the few things we do own is our true source of joy.

From establishing the ideal aesthetic in your home to pausing and saying a personal mantra before purchasing and receiving items, authenticity and intention will remain two guiding principles at the forefront of your minimalist practice. Now let us move on to the one area of your home that is so essential it requires exclusive attention: your wardrobe.

Curating Your Wardrobe

Although learning to curate my home with authenticity and intention has been beneficial, the area where these principles have made the biggest financial and time-saving impact is in my closet. Curating a functional minimalist wardrobe has literally transformed my  spending habits as well as my morning routine. In fact, it has allowed me to create what I like to call "a uniform life."

The Uniform Life

Now, let me preface by saying that the uniform life is not for everyone. Many of my dear friends are fashionistas who cannot imagine how I survive with a seasonal capsule wardrobe composed of only thirty-three items that I wear for three months (undergarments and workout clothing excluded). But it works for me, because despite my being nearly six feet tall and having spent my young adult years in the modeling industry, fashion is just not my thing. Do I like my clothing to look nice and provide comfort as I move from presenting in boardrooms to reading to children in classrooms? Absolutely. Can I wear the same clothing repeatedly without fear of judgment or feeling fashionably stunted? Also, absolutely.

In fact, I do!

Embracing a uniform lifestyle does not mean I wear the same pieces every single day. (However, many people also enjoy this capsule wardrobe approach. Perhaps one of the most famous faces of having an everyday uniform is Steve Jobs, who became well known for his simple black turtleneck and classic blue jeans.) My uniform life offers a bit more variety—it means that every season, my wardrobe is composed of thirty-three pieces that I know fit well while providing me with the confidence I need to look and feel my best. In addition to my infamous orange jumpsuit, I have several one-piece ensembles in my closet. The rationale? I find it incredibly frustrating pairing tops and bottoms. Having one-piece uniform ensembles makes my wardrobe (and life!) that much easier.

Even if you are not interested in adopting a daily or seasonal uniform, having a wardrobe that reflects your authentic style will be essential to maintaining your minimalist lifestyle. In addition to offering a bit of simplicity to the often frustrating "what should I wear" conundrum, knowing your authentic style helps inform your shopping and spending habits as a consumer. Similar to home design and décor, discovering what pieces and silhouettes work best for you makes shopping, or rather, not shopping, that much easier. You are less likely to buy clothing and accessories you will never wear.

What to Wear: Discovering Your Style

Ah, isn't it so easy to fall in love with fashion? Whether shopping online or in stores, many of us have found ourselves with an article of clothing, shoes, or accessories in our hands declaring our affection. But often, we are simply in awe of how beautiful something is or even with the idea of how it could make us look and feel beautiful. As we know, this love deepens when we touch items or try them on. And heaven forbid if salespeople or even fellow customers affirm how amazing something looks on us.

It's a wrap! Take my money!

But as you know, we often find these items languishing unworn in our closets or dressers.

As you work through your wardrobe to release attire that no longer serves you, the majority of what remains should be pieces that you love and wear regularly. These items are the first clues to discovering your authentic style. Are there more one-piece ensembles or do you enjoy mixing and matching your tops and bottoms? Do you gravitate toward the same bright colors and patterns, or are neutrals more your jam? What is it about these articles of clothing and accessories that you find so appealing you decided to keep them? Assessing the items that you already own is the simplest way to determine your authentic sense of style. Allow these pieces to be the foundation for your curated wardrobe.

Again, I recommend using the "need, use, love" philosophy when it comes to establishing your style. In addition to helping you begin building an ideal minimalist wardrobe, you can use this approach to regularly assess and manage your attire. Determining whether you still need, use, and love certain pieces will ensure you let go of what you rarely wear to make space for clothing that reflects your authentic style.

Maintaining Your Authentic Wardrobe

As you begin curating your wardrobe, one of the first steps you will have to take is learning how to manage it. Over the years I heard from many people who told me that they had no idea just how much stuff they owned until shelves or rods in their closets collapsed! Even after completing the "letting-go" process, many people find themselves struggling to manage their pared-down wardrobe. Why? Without a functional, organized closet you are unable to see what you actually have.

An Easy Way to Discover Your Personal Style

If I were to identify a pivotal moment in learning how to exercise the power of intention with my attire, it would be creating a capsule wardrobe through the Project 333 fashion challenge. I committed to select thirty-three items to wear over the span of three months. Of course, this forced me to be highly selective and as a result, my personal authentic style began to emerge. Now I have a solid wardrobe and occasionally purchase pieces to add to my seasonal capsules. But if you're not quite ready to jump into a three-month minimalist fashion challenge, there are many other minimalist fashion challenges that require less commitment, such as the 10x10 Fashion Challenge. Established by designer Lee "the Bee" Vosburgh, the concept is simple: Curate a mini–capsule closet of ten items that you work with for ten days to style your existing clothing to create new looks.

1. Pick any ten items from your current closet.
2. Style those items into ten different looks.
3. Use any ten days to do it.
4. Have fun and don't take it too seriously![1]

Simple, right? According to Bee, the 10x10 Fashion Challenge is for anyone who wants to: (1) take a break from shopping, (2) reinvest in their existing closet,

(3) test their style creativity, (4) make their closet work harder, (5) find a better sense of personal style, (6) test out a capsule closet, or (7) establish a couple of go-to uniforms.[2] Do any of these goals appeal to you? If so, give it a try! Even if you discover that capsule wardrobes and uniforms don't quite meet your fashion needs, trying this minimalist fashion challenge can help you uncover your authentic style.

Closet Organization

Although there are many organization systems and approaches to wardrobe management, none of them will work if your closet is not arranged in a way that is the most functional and controllable for you. When it comes to advice from leading practitioners, this is one area of mainstream minimalism where you will undoubtedly have to "take a little, keep a little." There is no point in investing in a system that will not be helpful. To underscore this point, let me share an aspect of my personal journey that involves one of the world's most beloved decluttering gurus: Marie Kondo.

Let me begin by saying that I love Marie Kondo. Her approach to decluttering has been integral to my personal practice. In fact, every season I "KonMari" my closet to assess what I need, use, and love to create my daily uniform and Project 333 capsule. However, there is one aspect of her organizational solutions that simply did not work for me, the one she is perhaps most renowned for: vertical folding. And it is not just vertical folding that does not work for me: It is folding, *period*!

During the acknowledgment phase of the "letting-go" process, I was surprised and overwhelmed by the amount of clothing I had stored in dressers, bins, and baskets (especially those with lids). This self-discovery led me to understanding that no matter how neatly I folded my clothes, if they went into certain storage solutions they very quickly became out of sight, out of mind.

As a result, I no longer own a dresser. Even my nightstands do not have drawers! Because now I know myself. If I want to keep track of just how much clothing I have and what I want to wear, the best organizational system for me is one where these items can hang in my closet so I can see them.

Managing a wardrobe without a dresser? Yes! I have two small boxes at the top of my closet to store small items such as undergarments, swimsuits, and socks. Everything else is on a hanger. Yes, even T-shirts. The few belongings I do fold are on open shelves in my closet where I can clearly see and access them. Otherwise, I run the risk of not being aware of what is in my wardrobe. This is an authentic approach to managing my wardrobe, and it continues to work well for *me*.

I will never forget how I felt discovering so many items in my wardrobe that I did not need. The first truth behind why they went unworn was I never needed them in the first place. But the second truth was equally as important—I had no way of seeing everything that I owned. As you begin to curate your wardrobe with intention, make sure you create an organizational system that will allow you store your belongings in a way that works best for you.

Buying New Things

Without a doubt, one of the most-asked questions when it comes to living with a minimalist wardrobe is "Can I buy new things?" Yes, of course you can. But you must be intentional about your purchases (or receiving of gifts) to ensure they align with your goals and authentic style. (This is probably a good time for me to reinforce my favorite personal mantra—"Remember, it's not a deal if you don't need it!")

Trust me, I get it. The temptation to purchase new items for our wardrobe is real. From being promoted at work and wanting to "look the part" to wanting to have social media–worthy photos for your upcoming vacation in the tropics, the allure of new items is never-ending. But unless you are intentional with your purchases (and what you choose to let go after you purchase them), you run the risk of starting over at Step One in the "letting-go" process and finding yourself, once again, acknowledging that you have more than you need.

Ask Yourself

1. Do I *need* this item?
2. Am I purchasing this item for a special occasion? Will I continue to *use* it for special occasions or just this occasion?
3. Does this item align with the goals that I have set for my curated minimalist wardrobe?
4. How will I feel if I don't buy this item?

5. Do I *love* this item or am I purchasing it for its perceived value (or how I will be perceived when I am wearing it)?

These are tough questions. But your honest answers will determine if you should proceed with making the purchase. Remember, discipline is an integral part of continuing your new lifestyle with less. But the reward is more disposable income, and a closet full of clothes you truly love.

With authenticity, intention, and discipline at the forefront of your decisions, maintaining your minimalist wardrobe will be much easier than you think. Start by creating a plan to assess your wardrobe regularly, whether monthly or seasonally. Ensure that formal wear is clearly visible, so you are less tempted to purchase attire you only need for one occasion (and consider borrowing formal wear from friends or using clothing rental services if you are concerned about repeat wears!). Knowing what is in your wardrobe—what works and what is missing—is the best way to remain focused on acquiring only what you need. Your decisions have an impact beyond your wardrobe. There is a trickle-down effect that is far reaching, extending from making an environmental impact and even to the people who create the items you wear. Understanding the true cost of fashion is also an essential aspect of minimalism.

Think Beyond Trends:
The True Cost of Fashion

For many people, fashion is more than just getting dressed, it is a way of life. Even though I am content wearing the same thirty-three items every season, many approach fashion the same way I do my literature collection—an abundance of favorites and classics nestled between the latest and greatest.

When it comes to clothing, many of the "latest and greatest" are trendy fashion that is inexpensive and made for the moment. Well, at least for a moment in one's closet. Quite often, when people are over one trend and on to the next, their fashionable inexpensive pieces are thrown in the trash or donated. Most of these items end up in landfills domestically or abroad, and there they remain for decades.

The Long Life Cycle of Fashion

The first time I was made aware of the longevity of clothing was during an environmental law class. Our discussion led to the sharing of a story about two young White men who frequently traveled to parts of Africa to sort through landfills. They had one objective: finding T-shirts and jeans from those "Save the World" campaigns that were so prevalent in the '80s. Upon discovering what they wanted, the two men returned to America to sell them at astronomical prices, because now, these articles were vintage.

I will be honest. My first thought was, *Ugh! Some White people just stay White peopling!*

My next thought was, *Wait. Clothing from the eighties is scattered throughout Africa in landfills? What the . . . ?*

Maybe I was naive, but until that moment, I had never given much thought to the clothes sent abroad in mass amounts during my childhood. It troubled me to know that some of my youthful attire was among them. So began my journey of learning more about donations and the life cycles of garments, which later expanded to understanding their cost to the environment from production to consumer. It was one of the reasons I cried during the acknowledgment phase of the "letting-go" process. Despite my best efforts to pay it forward, I knew my excess would be around for years to come.

"[The fashion industry] is incredibly wasteful and harmful to the environment."

—Stella McCartney

It is impossible to be a conscious consumer without understanding the true cost of your purchases. And I am not talking about price tags and shipping expenses. The true cost of clothing extends to everything from labor wages to environmental resources used to produce and manufacture products. Every item in your wardrobe costs far more than what you paid for it, especially when it comes to fast fashion.

Did You Know?

- It takes 715 gallons of water to produce the cotton needed for one T-shirt—that is almost three years' worth of drinking water.[3]
- It takes approximately 1,800 gallons of water to grow enough cotton to produce just one pair of jeans.[4]

- 1.3 trillion gallons of water are used each year for fabric dyeing alone.[5]

- Synthetic indigo dyes, which are derived from coal tar and toxic chemicals, are used in 90 percent of jeans made in China.[6]

- The cheapest type of denim dye is sulfur based, which is extremely damaging to the health of people exposed to it, and to the environment—it tends to remain in wastewater even after treatment.[7]

Being a conscious consumer is important when it comes to curating your wardrobe. Not only do you have to be intentional, but you also must be mindful of the true cost of the garment that you are purchasing. The lower the price tag, the higher the cost of environmental impact and the lower the wages of the person who created it.

Fast fashion isn't as cheap as you think it is.

Sustainable Fashion: Worth the Price

Whenever I mention sustainable fashion in minimalist workshops, one person inevitably declares, "The pieces are beautiful but so expensive!" Yes, it's true: Sustainable clothing has a higher price tag. But it is important to understand why.

Labor

According to Rebecca Van Bergen, founder and director of Nest, a nonprofit dedicated to increasing global workforce awareness and inclusivity, the predominant factor for the higher price tags on sustainable fashion is labor. Bangladesh is one of the cheapest places for brands to manufacture their garments, and as a result, it is the second-largest exporter of fashion to the United States. Curious to know the legal minimum wage for a Bangladesh garment worker? It is $94 a month, a far cry from the $191 a month needed to provide a family with basic living expenses. When labor is done in countries with stronger labor protections, a portion of the higher labor costs and production is passed down to the consumer.

Materials

Despite what many people might think, there are few options for brands to consider when it comes to high-quality materials that meet the best standards for ethics and sustainability. And the closer brands get to the source of raw materials—such as purchasing cotton buds directly from the farmer—the higher the cost of the end garment for the manufacturer and, ultimately, the consumer. When it comes to fashion, materials matter—from being free from harmful dyes to cost per wear. Unlike fast-fashion items that are meant to be worn one or two times, garments that are made from high-quality, sustainable materials are meant to last for years. Yes, the initial cost may be on the high end. But you can be assured that you purchased a garment you can wear for an extended period without needing to replace it.

Certifications

Due to increasingly regulated standards in the fashion industry, if brands want to declare that they are ethical and sustainable, they must prove it. One of the reasons for the higher price tags on sustainable fashion is that you are sharing the cost (and benefiting from!) brands who have taken the extra step to obtain certifications to verify they meet strict ethical standards. The verification process also includes regular audits of garment factories to ensure workers are not subject to inhumane conditions. An additional benefit is that many fair labor standard certification organizations use a portion of their fees to establish funds for garments workers to access for various purposes.

Scale of Production

In addition to paying lower wages and using cheaper materials, one of the reasons fast fashion is so cheap is that brands produce mass amounts of garments (even if there is no demand!). As in most industries, when garments are produced in bulk the cost per item is lower, and sometimes even fixed per month. In comparison, ethical fashion is often made to order or produced in small batches. This approach is good for the environment—it reduces waste as well as disposal of unpurchased items. When you purchase an ethical, sustainable garment, you are also paying for small-scale production such as the wages for the seamstress who hand-sewed your clothing.

Direct-to-Consumer

Most fast-fashion brands follow the traditional wholesale model. They sell their garments to a wholesale distributor who then sells the clothing to consumers (and keeps a portion of the sale). Sustainable brands use a direct-to-consumer model where they sell their garments online or in their brick-and-mortar store. But this model requires brands to invest in their sales infrastructure to ensure their business runs smoothly. Whenever I purchase a garment from an ethical, sustainable brand, I take pride in knowing that I am supporting their business and approach to producing ethical fashion.

Transparency

Because sustainable fashion brands must meet so many strict standards, there is an added benefit to consumers that may not be readily apparent: transparency. When you purchase sustainable garments, you know exactly *why* you are paying a higher cost. Unlike buying a luxury item where you are likely paying for the logo, rest assured that when you purchase a sustainable garment you are paying for an ethically made, high-quality product.

> "If a company is exploiting people and the planet to ensure low prices and a quick turnaround, is the clothing really cheaper?"
>
> —Leah Thomas, *The Good Trade*

Looking to avoid the high costs of purchasing sustainable clothing? Simply avoid buying new things! Consider curating your intentional wardrobe by purchasing clothing from consignment shops and thrift stores. There is an abundance of clothing available that need loving homes. Whenever I acquire gently worn or barely worn items, I think of my friend Céline Semaan's tagline and say, "This is good for the earth and good for the people."

You can also repurpose your clothing and accessories by allowing friends to come "shop" at your house. Because I curate my wardrobe seasonally, there are always a few items that I am

FOR THE CULTURE
▼▲▼▲▼

Let's keep it 100—the Black community takes pride in looking and smelling good. It is one of the reasons why we are the most targeted population when it comes to sales and marketing. When it comes to Black consumerism, the level of spending compared to income and earning potential is astounding. Despite being in the lowest income bracket, Black Americans are the highest consumers of virtually every retail sector. And this truth comes at a cost not only to our wallets and the environment, but also to future generations.

One of the most startling statistics I came across while researching the Tulsa Race Riots was how quickly dollars earned are spent outside of our community. Tulsa was once home to the Greenwood District, one of the wealthiest communities of its time, before it was destroyed in 1921. In its heyday, Black dollars circulated within Greenwood for almost an entire year before leaving the community. Presently, our dollars leave our community within six hours.

A dollar circulates:

- 6 hours in the Black community
- 17 days in the White community
- 20 days in the Jewish community
- 30 days in the Asian community

As the most active consumers we have a responsibility to ourselves, our communities, and our descendants to use our dollars more wisely. Looking to curb your spending and consumption? Consider committing to a "No Spend Month" once a year or quarterly. And whenever you do make purchases, consider taking an extra step to buy from Black makers and creators. In this way, at least your consumption benefits your community.

willing to part with (I store my favorites so they can make another appearance in their respective seasons!). There is nothing like seeing the joy on my friends' faces as they sort through clothing to discover pieces that can meet their needs. Bonus: receiving texts or being tagged in posts by your friends proudly rocking their new gear!

Consignment, thrifting, and clothing swaps are just a few ways to practice being a conscious consumer. If you absolutely must purchase new, consider the true cost of the item you're buying—from the laborers who made it to the environmental impact.

Remember, the true cost of fashion extends well beyond price tags.

Words of Wisdom: Elim Chu

Elim Chu is a curious creative professional with innate skills in finding meaning within the seemingly simple. Throughout her work, she helps people understand the true life span of their objects and actions. Elim was one of the first people to welcome me to the online minimalist community, and I continue to be inspired by her dedication to helping others understand the importance of sustainable fashion and benefits of being a mindful consumer.

I was thirty years old when I discovered I owned over one hundred pairs of shoes.

I was taking the leap into marriage. My partner and I had found our first apartment together: a mid-century low-rise building with original wood floors, lots of natural light, and... minimal storage. Five hundred square feet with *only* two full-sized closets—that I had to share. Expletive!

The charming and oh-so-small apartment couldn't house my now enormous wardrobe. I had to pare down. As it turns out you can learn a lot about yourself when sorting through hundreds of pieces of clothing. It was easy to see how my lifetime of chasing the approval of my peers—be it my fellow fashion stylists, or my White school friends—and living up to the hopes and sacrifices of my Chinese immigrant parents, who wanted to give me more, had led to a closet overflowing with impulse purchases.

In choosing to be curious about the clothes I put on my body, I found myself on the most unexpected path of discovery: Shopping is so much more than filling a closet or desire.

I learned how my shopping habits factored in capitalism and could be a tool in decolonization. That my ability to choose is a privilege not afforded to all, power I continue to learn how to wield. The *global retail market* had sales of approximately 24 trillion U.S. dollars in 2018. How we shop for our wardrobes can affect communities—online and offline, locally and globally.

It turns out there is no perfect way to be a conscious consumer. Mindful clothing choices will look and feel different for everyone, and the comparison game is futile here, too. Choices live on a spectrum. For every purchase, there is a light and dark side to consider, acknowledge, and accept. Before I add new pieces to my wardrobe, I often ask whether an item can be purchased through a local maker or business owner, or whether it could be purchased secondhand instead, but maybe you need to focus on how much you can spend on this choice.

Whenever I'm really unsure about a purchase, I wait it out. Sometimes it's just a crush, feelings for something shiny and new, that fizzles overnight.

No matter what, trust your gut. No one knows you, your needs, or your style better than *you*.

What you need, use, and love is constantly changing. Regularly assessing your belongings as well as being mindful of what you purchase will be essential to maintaining your personal practice. And don't be surprised if you frequently discover items that you once thought you had to keep but are now willing to let go of. This *is* a journey.

Less Is Liberation

As a Black woman in constant pursuit of redis-covering and reimagining ways to thrive and not just survive, I have found a true sense of purpose and freedom in my decision to live with less. And although I love being known as  the Afrominimalist, had I known then what I know now, I might have chosen a different moniker. Because the term "minimalism" remains misunderstood and as a result, people may disregard this lifestyle as another passing trend rather than embrace it as an opportunity to live a more fulfilling life.

As you now know, living with less is about more than just having a tidy home. It is a mindset, a personal commitment to be a more conscious consumer. It is a process of self-discovery that teaches you to be honest and intentional about what you want and allow into your life. Only you know what you need in order to have a fulfilling life, and once you discover this, you can define your minimalist practice in alignment with your truth.

"Living with less is not only liberating, less *is* liberation."

—Christine

Choosing to embrace the practice of minimalism has afforded me more time to write, to nap, to daydream. It has allowed me to create a life that I love, one that is full of passion and purpose. I choose my projects with intention rather than accept work as a means to end. For me, living with less allows me to enjoy a most liberating existence. And it is a lifestyle that is attainable for anyone willing to pursue it.

FOR THE CULTURE

▼▲▼▲▼

Considering a life with less when we've been constantly encouraged to acquire more requires a serious shift in perspective, priorities, and purpose. Remember this is your life, not a race, and most important, remember there are many different ways that minimalism can look and feel, and that the only sure way your practice will be successful is if you do minimalism your way. Allow other Black minimalists to inspire you and encourage you throughout your journey. Understand and remember the benefits of living with less are so much more than what mainstream minimalism portrays. Your new lifestyle is an opportunity for continued growth and development, personally, financially, and professionally. Living with less is a way for you to achieve liberation on your terms.

keep going, keep growing

There are so many stories from people who have decluttered their homes many times, only to fill them back up. That is why we had to unearth the root causes of your consumption, not just clean up and organize the resulting leaves. You cannot continue to pluck the leaves and never look at the roots. And trust me, whatever roots you have left untouched will unearth themselves over time.

I also want you to know that you may have setbacks, moments where you find yourself returning to your old habits and behaviors. And if and when you do, remember one of the most vital steps in the process: forgiveness. You will know the reasons for your decisions and, more

important, you now know the process to course correct. The only way to be successful in your journey to minimalism is to keep going.

When it comes to living with less, I liken the lifelong commitment to a recording. There may be moments where you must rewind and return to your past, or even moments when you have to pause. Just remember to press play again. Don't ever stop.

Maintaining your personal practice will require a lot of self-assessment and discipline. Undoubtedly, this will include having some uncomfortable but necessary conversations with the people you love. You will need to let family and friends know of your intentions to maintain your new lifestyle. You will need to respectfully ask that they support your decision by refraining from buying, gifting, and placing expectations on you to acquire things.

If you are married or partnered, you will have to ask for support from your closest loved one. And you may find this especially challenging if everyone in your household is not interested in living with less. Therefore, you may have to make some compromises. And you may have to ask your closest loved one to make some concessions as well.

Living with less will require you to be honest—with yourself and others. You will have to learn patience and exercise restraint as you learn to navigate your new lifestyle. And now is the time to extend to yourself the grace we acknowledged at the start of your journey to minimalism. You will not get it right every single time. And that is why the only way to be successful is to just keep going.

Minimalism Is the Gift of Liberation

There are many lessons you will learn along your journey to minimalism. Some of these experiences are applicable to the larger minimalist community, such as discovering the power of authenticity and intention. Others will be special, profound moments of self-discovery that are just for you. But there is one takeaway that is significant to all of us: Minimalism is a way to liberate yourself from things that no longer serve you, behaviors that do not benefit you, and expectations that do not align with your personal mission and vision.

Learning your power as a consumer—both with your spending and consumption—frees you from the societal standards that so many of us find overbearing and stressful. Minimalism allows you to discover that one of the truest forms of joy is not acquiring things, but rather developing meaningful relationships and having time and resources for experiences that you can enjoy in the moment and reflect on for years to come. This liberation is empowering! You will curate your home and wardrobe differently. You will spend your dollars more consciously and pursue your goals and dreams more passionately. Throughout your journey of living with less, you will continuously discover the benefits of maintaining a life on your terms. You will be intentional in the pursuit of your happiness—the most liberating gift of all.

Words of Wisdom: Jewel Pearson

Jewel Pearson is not only a well-known advocate in the tiny house community, she is the first Black woman who taught me and so many others how important representation is in the minimalist and tiny house movements. Jewel's 360-square-foot tiny house is nothing short of a dream and has been featured on several national and global platforms. But it's not only Jewel's living space that impresses. It was her words, "Living with less is freedom," as we stood in a cotton field in North Carolina, that resonated with me most. Jewel taught me that less is liberation and the time for liberation is now.

My "journey" to living in a tiny house began in the early '90s. Being a young, single, Black mom is hard, but I was determined to defy negative statistics and society's biased narratives for what our story would be.

My dream was that once my daughter was an adult, I'd be able to live an easier life, one that felt lighter than the heaviness I was often experiencing. A life that would allow me to make decisions  based on desires and wants, instead of always having to make decisions based on needs and determined by finances. I would live in a RV full-time and there would be no permanent address—I wanted to live and know freedom.

In the ten years after my daughter went to college, I downsized my possessions and spaces to eventually living in a one-bedroom/one-bath apartment. I also pivoted from my dream of RV living to the plan of building a tiny house, and in October 2014, I purchased my customized trailer (the foundation of my tiny house) and finished the build in late May 2015. Someone told me just as I'd started the process that building a house ranks highly on the list of life's most stressful events and no truer words have been spoken. It didn't help that I didn't have any prior experience with building, nor that the build was being filmed to be featured on HGTV's *Tiny House, Big Living* show.

It was never lost on me during my research, planning, and build that I didn't see anyone else in the movement who looked like me, but that never impacted my plan to be part of it. That had also been my experience growing up in my classrooms, so I was used to it. What I naively didn't consider, though, was how different my journey would be in comparison to my counterparts': I didn't foresee that I'd have to relocate my tiny house twice due to the dangers of racism or that my pictures would be so triggering to some that they'd garner racist social media messages or that my speaking out about my experiences would warrant anonymous threatening messages in response. I also didn't consider what the impact would be for other Black and brown people as they FINALLY saw a Black person in the tiny house movement when my HGTV episode aired. Representation matters, it matters a lot.

One of my first messages I received after my HGTV episode aired was from an older Black woman who expressed how proud she was to see me in the movement and she shared that she thought I was the "Harriet Tubman of tiny houses." While this woman and I both respectfully know that I haven't done a fragment of anything as important, meaningful, and/or dangerous as she, her will to know that freedom she was fighting for resonates with me and receiving that message made me so proud, I was honored. In the illustrious words of Harriet Tubman, "Don't ever stop. Keep going. If you want a taste of freedom, keep going."

Minimalism is true liberation, and I am excited that you have chosen a lifestyle that can afford you the freedom to discover what matters most. Forget the number of items you think you need to own. Avoid giving in to the idea that minimalism means a life devoid of colors, textures, and interesting textiles. Renounce the belief that there is only one way to live with less. This is minimalism *your* way, and you are in for the most beautiful, liberating journey of a lifetime.

"Living small is simple.
Living small is smart.
Living small is responsible."

—Laura Fenton, *The Little Book of Living Small*

It is my hope that you embrace and pursue your new lifestyle of less with confidence because you are more than equipped to be successful in this endeavor. Remember the lessons that you have learned, and the beautiful discoveries that you have already uncovered. Remember not only the power of authenticity and intention, but also the power in your self-reflections, which will help you stay grounded in your intentions and on track with your goals. And always remember, it's not a deal if you don't need it.

Guiding Lights to Live with Less

 I would be remiss to leave you without a few words of wisdom and a bit of additional guidance as you continue your journey to minimalism. I created ten affirmations to serve as guiding lights as you embark upon your personal practice.

Over the years I have learned the value of adding "I will" to the beginning of any personal aspirations. These two simple words underscore an undeniable level of determination and commitment. That is why, instead of declaring your willingness to "try," I begin each of the guiding lights with these two powerful words. You will live with less, and I am excited about how this decision will change and benefit your life.

TEN GUIDING LIGHTS

1. I will commit to becoming conscious of what I own and what I buy.

2. I will acknowledge when I have more than I need.

3. I will learn why I have more than I need.

4. I will forgive myself for past spending habits and forgive my caretakers for their lessons and expectations.

5. I will let go of what no longer serves me.

6. I will pay it forward by donating items that can serve others.

7. I will choose authenticity over aesthetics.

8. I will only own things that I need, use, and love.

9. I will commit to the journey, not the destination.

10. I will continue to learn ways to live with intention.

I am still in the midst of my journey. I am *still* letting go of things that no longer serve me as I continue to learn what it means to need, use, and love things and, one day, release them. I am still making self-discoveries that continue to enhance my minimalist practice and expand on my liberation. I am still growing, and growth will forever remain a part of personal mantra and practice.

"I am not a grown woman. I am a growing woman.
And may I always be growing, never fully grown."
—Christine

As I continue my journey as the Afrominimalist, as I continue to learn the joy and freedom of living with less, I am still growing. And this is exactly how I want to experience life—always growing, never grown.

May we continue to learn and grow together as we choose to live with intention.

In Minimalist Solidarity,

The Afrominimalist

acknowledgments

When I sat down to acknowledge the beautiful village who helped make *The Afrominimalist's Guide to Living with Less* possible, I never planned to start with thanking a mouse. But then again, I shouldn't be surprised. Shouting out a mouse for helping me write a book beyond my wildest dreams is so on brand for 2020.

Ah, 2020. The year that required me to spend more time at home than ever before. Which inevitably led to me hoarding snacks in my bedroom. Which led to a mouse finding those goodies while simultaneously leaving behind a few things of his own: fleas. Which led to a total disruption in my life in the midst of a pandemic while struggling to write this book. It might seem a bit weird to say that I'm grateful.

But I am.

Because the situation taught me so much about myself and more importantly, I learned just how solid, strong, and supportive my village is. Going through such hardship allowed me to me to fully understand and appreciate the depth of the love my community has for me. I learned that I could call my wonderful agent,

209

Emily Sylvan Kim, day or night at any time to talk about anything. From lamenting about being displaced by fleas to reading sections of the book aloud, Emily is more than my agent—she is a dear friend. And I am forever grateful for her wise guidance and counsel.

That my brilliant, sweet editor, Hannah Robinson, is not only kind, gracious, and understanding but also compassionate. Which is also needed but was especially needed in 2020. She shares my love for both long hours, hilarious gifs and memes, and other shenanigans. Somehow, Hannah had the ability to pull the most beautiful story out of me that discusses one of the most difficult periods of my life. *The Afrominimalist's Guide to Living with Less* would not be what it is today without her steadfast belief in my words, work ethic, and constant encouragement.

Along with Emily and Hannah, the Afrominimalist home team included my I-don't-know-what-I-would-do-without-her executive assistant, Ellen Brescia, and my high-school-classmate-turned-dear-friend and brand strategist, Charisma McAdams. Truly a dream team, and together we discovered the truth behind the familiar adage: teamwork makes the dream work.

The Afrominimalist's Guide to Living with Less came alive with Octavia Thorn's beautiful illustrations, which are actually xilografía—every image was carved backwards on wooden blocks. And it is laced with loving words of wisdom from dear friends who are leaders in the intentional living, sustainability, and design sectors: Jewel Pearson, Elim Chu, Nicole Crowder, Courtney Carver, Laura Alice Fenton, Pia Henderson, and Chanae Richards (who has become my dear sister and is also a master flea fighter!)

Thank you also to everyone at Tiller, including but not limited to Theresa DiMasi, Anja Schmidt, Lauren Ollerhead, Laura Flavin, and Molly Pieper. You are truly all a dream publisher and thank you so much for supporting me. Thank you also to Nicole Dewey who is absolutely phenomenal.

Of course, few writers truly write alone. Especially Black writers. We are family, members of a tightknit community of like minds and kindred spirits beyond our creative endeavors. I would not be the writer I am today without my peers, and I most certainly appreciate their love and support (i.e., listening to me complain without judgment) while writing *The Afrominimalist's Guide to Living with Less*. There is no way I can name the entire village, because there are so many brothers and sisters in my writing family. But I would be remiss to not acknowledge and give big love to the Rhode Island Writers Colony especially Jill Louise Busby, Johnalynn Holland, Madhuri Pavamani, and the Colony's Creative Director, Jason Reynolds, as these four people were pivotal to supporting me in 2020. Thank you for listening to me, pushing and challenging me, and holding me accountable. We are truly blessed to have each other in this wild, unpredictable world. And we are fortunate to have Eaton DC as a place to write, gather, break bread, and crack jokes.

I would also be remiss to not shout-out my pandemic crew, the people who I relied on for love, laughter, and everything in between: Julye Williams, Catherine Wigginton Greene, Joe Patrick II, Malini Ranganathan, Shajmil Smith, Sheldon Scott, and Rachel Cargle. And of course, those folks who played multiple roles in addition to being in my social bubble: Chanae, Emily, and Jason. Thank you for uplifting and sustaining me through such difficult, unprecedented times—ready for some precedented times!

Lastly, to my beautiful mother and daughter, thank you both believing in me, for supporting, for reminding me that I have been called to important work throughout the African diaspora. I appreciate the sacrifices you've made to make my work possible. No one makes me laugh harder or gives me more joy than my girls, my two best friends. I love y'all so much!

And thank you to *you* for reading *The Afrominimalist's Guide to Living with Less.* I am forever grateful to the Afrominimalist community and all the memories we've already made together. Let's keep going, let's keep growing. Because as we know, less is liberation. So, let's get free!

Love,
Christine

notes

WELCOME TO THE JOURNEY

1. "Updated: How Do Black People Spend Their Money? (The Racial Wealth Gap)," BlackMenInAmerica.com, August 20, 2020, https://blackmeninamerica.com/updated-how-do-black-people-spend-their-money-3/.
2. Ibid.
3. Ibid.

MEET YOUR GUIDE

1. Although this is a term I use regularly, it is certainly not one that I am claiming to be the originator of. Throughout the African diaspora, it is quite common for people to use "Afro" as a prefix to denote cultural influence of a predominately White ideal or action.

WHY YOU HAVE MORE THAN YOU NEED

1. Mary MacVean, "For Many People, Gathering Possessions Is Just the Stuff of Life," *Los Angeles Times*, March 21, 2014, https://www.latimes.com/health/la-xpm-2014-mar-21-la-he-keeping-stuff-20140322-story.html.

2. U.S. Census Bureau.

3. Mary MacVean, "For Many People."

4. Ibid.

5. Megan DeMatteo, "The Average American Has $90,460 in Debt—Here's How Much Debt Americans Have at Every Age," CNBC.com, January 22, 2021.

6. Ibid.

7. Ibid.

8. Ibid.

9. Joanna Piacenza, "Black Consumers More Likely Than the Public to Look to Celebrities When Buying," Morning Consult, February 21, 2020, https://morningconsult.com/2020/02/21/black-consumers -brands-celebrities-influencers/.

10. Antonio Moore, "America's Financial Divide: The Racial Breakdown of U.S. Wealth in Black and White," *HuffPost*, April 13, 2015, https:// www.huffpost.com/entry/americas-financial-divide_b_7013330.

11. Josh Harkinson, "America's 100 Richest People Control More Wealth than the Entire Black Population," *Mother Jones*, December 2, 2015, https://www.motherjones.com/politics/2015/12/report-100-people -more-wealth-african-american-population/.

12. Antonio Moore, "#BlackWealthMatters: The 5 Largest U.S. Landowners Own More Land than All Black America Combined," *HuffPost*, October 28, 2015, https://www.huffpost.com/entry/ted-turner-owns -nearly-14_b_8395448.

13. Joshua Holland, "The Average Black Family Would Need 228 Years to Build the Wealth of a White Family Today," *Nation*, August 8, 2016, https://www.thenation.com/article/archive/the-average-black-family -would-need-228-years-to-build-the-wealth-of-a-white-family- today/.

14. "Updated: How Do Black People Spend Their Money? (The Racial Wealth Gap)," BlackMenInAmerica.com, August 20, 2020, https://

blackmeninamerica.com/updated-how-do-black-people-spend-their
-money-3/.

15. Henry Louis Gates Jr., PBS, "The African Americans: Many Rivers to
Cross," PBS.org.

PART TWO: THE PROCESS

1. Understanding Poverty, World Bank, WorldBank.org.
2. Ibid.

A LESSON IN INTENTION

1. The 10x10 Fashion Challenge: https://www.stylebee.ca/10-x-10
-challenge/#10-about.
2. Ibid.
3. https://www.thefashionlaw.com/how-many-gallons-of-water-does-it
-take-to-make-a-single-pair-of-jeans/.
4. Ibid.
5. Ibid.
6. https://www.theguardian.com/environment/2015/dec/27/eco-guide
-the-green-jeans.
7. http://www.uvm.edu/~shali/Levi.pdf.

about the author

Christine Platt is a modern-day Renaissance woman. From serving as an advocate for policy reform to using the power of storytelling as a tool for social change, Christine's work reflects her practice of living with intention. She holds a BA in Africana studies, MA in African-American studies, and a JD in general law. Christine has written more than two dozen literary works for people of all ages. When she's not writing, Christine spends her time curating *The Afrominimalist*—a creative platform chronicling her journey to minimalism. Visit her online at TheAfrominimalist.com.